Ye Olde Seafaring Lexicon

being
a Provisional Collection of
Seamanship Jargon, Argot, Cant,
Patois, Slang, Figures of Speech,
Lingua Franca & Other Vernacular Idiolects
as well as Several Philosophical, Idiomatic
& Singular Terms of Particular Consequence
to the Question of Maritime Venture

Ye Olde Seafaring Lexicon

They that go down to the sea in ships, that do business in great waters;

These see the works of the LORD, and his wonders in the deep.

For he commandeth, and raiseth the stormy wind, which lifteth up the waves thereof.

They mount up to the heaven, they go down again to the depths: their soul is melted because of trouble.

They reel to and fro, and stagger like a drunken man, and are at their wit's end.

Then they cry unto the LORD in their trouble, and he bringeth them out of their distresses.

He maketh the storm a calm, so that the waves thereof are still.

Then are they glad because they be quiet; so he bringeth them unto their desired haven.

Oh that men would praise the LORD for his goodness, and for his wonderful works to the children of men!

Psalm 107

aback [be taken aback] a dangerous situation when the wind veers or backs so it is on the wrong side of the sails, pressing them back against the mast and forcing the ship to suddenly slow, often with drastic consequences

abaft toward the stern, aft

'abandon ship!' an unambiguous command of urgency

able seaman a knowledgeable sailor

aboard on ship, or, alongside ship [Presently a canoe came aboard the man-o-war.]

above board on deck, too, a compliment to or about a trustworthy sailor [Aye, he's above board, captain, sure as day.]

abroach to open a pipe of wine

action boarding, or, broadside fighting

Act of Grace [Act of Pardon or King's Pardon] a royal act pardoning any pirate who promises to cease plundering, his past acts as a pirate forgiven

Adamastor a hideous beast who forewarns sailors of disaster if they will not seek another route

addled confused [That wind o' ball at first addled Long Jack, and then took the wind fro his sails altogether.]

addlepate a fool

afore the front of any ocean-going craft

after [aft] situated at the stern

aftercastle the stern or back of the ship

afterdeck the part of the deck abaft midships

afterguard a body of men at work on the quarterdeck and poop

ague the chills caused by severe fever [Ach! Ol' Slim Josey hast the ague!]

Ye Olde Seafaring Lexicon

ahoy! the hailing of another ship [Ahoy, mates! or Ship ahoy!]

albatross a large seabird of good omen to sailors, an omen of bad weather if seen flying round a ship mid-ocean, unlucky to kill one because it embodies the soul of a dead mariner, frequently killed to make tobacco pouches from its webbed feet, and often with the expected disastrous circumstances occurring

a-lee towards the lee

all at sea in a state of confusion and disorder

'all hands ahoy!' [on deck] the command to have every sailor above board

aloft above deck, in the masts and rigging

'aloft and furl!' the command to climb aloft and furl, or fold, all sails

Alv Erlingsson a Norwegian baron born ca. 1190 in Tornberg, Norderhov, Buskerud, commits innumerable acts of piracy throughout his life including seizing and robbing German vessels, making an attack on Duke Håkon, the younger brother of the Norwegian king, and attacking Denmark, is eventually exiled for his acts

amain immediately, or, lower your topsails, or if spoke to an enemy, signifies yield [Amain and prepare to be boarded!]

amidships any point in the middle of a ship

anchors aweigh said in preparation of getting underway

ancien regime [French] the dominant paradigm

angel-shot chain shot, so named because those hit by it soon see angels

Anne Dieu-Le-Veut [Marie-Anne or Marianne] born ca. 1650, a French buccaneer, her name meaning 'Anne Gods-wants-it' since she has a will so strong that if she wants something, it is as if God wants it

Ye Olde Seafaring Lexicon

anti-guggler a tube [reed or cane] feloniously slipped into the Navy captain's private stock to suck out the contents

apple cheeked bow a broad, apple-shaped bow allowing a ship to carry heavy gunnery without pitching deeply forward

'apprehend danger from a wind blowin' from the same quarter' to be informed on by companions already in gaol [jail]

apprentices indentured servants of officers-turned-pirate, usually acquitted when apprehended if no evidence comes forth that they have willfully taken part in the sharing of booty

'a qualm of conscience came athwart his stomach' literally, 'He was suddenly sorry for his actions.'

archery a common battle tactic for Elizabethan Sea Dogs

'armed to the teeth' a saying describing the praxis of the common outlaw routinely carrying so much weaponry that the only place left for an additional knife lies between his teeth

armorer smithy, blacksmith, prized alongside the carpenter aboardship

arrack [West Indian] an alcohol made from rice or cocoa [coco] sap

'as good as fifty men more' the Black Flag

ashore off ship

astern behind

'as the crow flies' a crow released at sea will fly straight toward the nearest land, caged crows are kept aboard to assist in unsure navigational situations

astrolabe a wheel-like contraption which measures the Sun's height to determine latitude

athwart any direction across the line of a ship's course, or, across

athwartships at a right angle to the midline or centerline of the ship

'at loggerheads' at odds with, at war with

aulin an Arctic gull which terrifies other seabirds by racing at them at breakneck speed, and then eats their vomit

Auster the South Wind

Avalon [Welsh: Ynys Yr Afallon] a paradise lying in the Western Sea beyond the Ninth Wave

avast beware, stop, halt, hold an operation [Avast, ye sea dogs!]

Awilda the daughter of a 5th century Scandinavian king who arranged a marriage for her to Alf, the crown prince of Denmark, refuses her father's choice, so she and some of her female friends dress like sailors and commandeer a ship, taking it into the Baltic as a way of escape, while sailing, they come across a pirate ship which has recently lost its captain, the girls hold out valiantly in the ensuing fight, because four days later the pirates vote her their new captain, her newly acquired crew enjoys great success in purchase and are eventually noticed by most of Scandinavia, the King of Denmark sends his son, her betrothed, and his finest warriors out to battle with her and her pirates, Prince Alf and his men are able to board her ship and gain the upper hand in the battle, she is so taken with the courage of the prince that she stops the battle, reveals her true identity, and agrees to marry Alf

awning a sail set up like a canopy to prevent the scorching of the Sun

axe [hatchet] a common piratical weapon, and during the signing of ship's articles often sworn upon instead of the Bible, too used to cut lines, knock down cabin doors, and sometimes to cut the masts or yards on a ship

B

baboon watch the unfortunate watch while the rest of the crew is off duty and ashore, usually assigned to the youngest crew member

back the wind when it changes contrary to normal pattern [The wind's back, captain!]

back and fill to work the sails so as to alternately fill and empty them of wind, a technique of tacking employed when the tide is with the ship but the wind against it, too used when maneuvering in a narrow space

backstaff the forerunner of the sextant

baize woolen or cotton fabric napped to imitate felt

bale to lade water out of the ship's hold

ballast a heavy substance used to improve stability and control the draft of a ship, made of pig iron, stones, or gravel

bangkong [Indonesian] the preferred vessel of the feared Sea Dyaks

Banner of King Death the black pirate flag, often depicted with a skeleton holding an hourglass, or with a pirate or a skeleton dancing round, but more commonly emblazoned with a skull and crossbones, allegedly based on the Irish nursery-bogie Rawhead Bloodybones, but too thought to be inspired by the death's head entered in the captain's log when a seaman dies

bar a sandbank or shoal in the mouth of a harbor or river

Barbarossa [Latin: Redbeard] fierce Turkish corsair of the Mediterranean during the late 15th century

Barbary States the countries of Morocco, Algiers, Tunis, and Tripoli, in large part controlled by pirates

barca-longa [Spanish: barco luengo] a large Spanish

fishing boat having two or three masts and employed for coastal trading and occasional offshore fishing, too, a longboat

bare boles bare masts

'bare up the helm!' the command to head home

barnacle entering the English language ca. the mid-1300s, but not referring to the marine crustaceans adhering to the hulls of wooden ships removed by careening the vessel several times each year, rather, the name given to a type of goose thought to hatch from the shell of a crustacean because no one knows where its breeding grounds are [He be 'Barnacle Bill', mate, for we know not his original.]

barque [French: bark] any small vessel before the 18th century, later, a ship having three masts, the first two square-rigged and the third, or aft mast, being fore-and aft rigged, a fast ship with shallow draft and a favorite of Caribbean pirates, holds a complement of ca. 90 maximum, large enough to hold a longboat, a cutter, and a surf-boat

barquentine [French: barkentine] three- or more-masted ship square-rigged on the foremast and fore-and-aft rigged on both masts

barrack stanchion a sailor in comfortable post ashore

barrel [be over a barrel] a sailor about to be flogged is tied either to a grating, one of the masts, or over the barrel of a deck cannon, thus, by extension, to corner somebody with a question he or she has no knowledge to answer [Ye've got me o'er a barrel on that one, sirrah!]

bar shot two halves of a round shot joined by a rigid bar, fired against rigging, etc.

'batten down Olde hatches' to secure the ship's hull and deck openings [hatches] to prevent entry of water and air, thus, a command to prepare for trouble

Ye Olde Seafaring Lexicon

'batten yer hatch!' shut your mouth

batteries armaments along a settlement's coastal walls

beak the bow of a ship

beam the extreme width of a ship at her widest part [We wast knocked onto beam ends!]

bear a hand offer help

bear away to change direction to sail before the wind

bear down [1] to approach another ship from to windward, or from downwind, thus effectively cutting off their wind

bear down [2] the command to cease sail and drop anchor, usually issued from an enemy ship [Strike yer colors and bear down!]

bear off from to stand further off or away from land, or away from another ship as in fending off

bear too to sail before the wind [wind filling the sails]

bear up a command to sail closer to the wind or closer to the direction the wind is blowing, by extension, 'Don't give up' [We bore up under Cap'n Nagg, but 'twas ne'er a fine day 'neath his lethal eye.]

bear with land to approach nearer to land

bearded the condition of a ship which has not been careened of late

beat to sail against the wind

beat home return to home port [An' that's when we beat home to our dalilahs.]

beating up sailing against the wind, especially on alternate tacks

beauty an affectionate [or derogatory] name for any sailor [Batten yer hatch, me beauty, an' pay a mind to the dooty at hand.]

becalm blanketing another ship by cutting off her wind either with one's own ship or by forcing her into proximity to land

Ye Olde Seafaring Lexicon

beer always on board and imbibed in preference to the unsafe water, allowed on and off duty in the Navy and on merchants, with drunkenness being the responsibility of the sailor drinking

before a wind [before the wind] when a wind is behind a ship's sails

before the mast the position of seamen working and living in the forecastle or fok'sl

be in Davy's grip to be close to death, or frightened

be in the offing a good, safe distance from shore and barely visible from land

belay to secure any rope, or, to cease some action or dangerous word [Belay that, sirrah!]

belaying pins short lengths of wood, iron, or brass set up around the ship and used to belay rigging, too, a common pirate weapon in hand-to-hand combat

'belay that yarn!' stop lying

bells the strokes on the ship's bell to mark the passage of time on board ship

belly wind filling sails [When the sails belly we'll be fully under way, sir!]

belly timber food, victuals

bend a knot used to join two ropes, lines, or cables to one another or to an object, such as an anchor's shackle, a knot, more properly, usually involves untwisting the individual strands of a rope for the purpose of tucking them under and over one another to make a Stopper Knot or a Turk's Head or similar knot

Benjamin Hornigold an English pirate during the early 18th century ravaging the New World, like many Caribbean pirates, he serves previously on an English privateer during the War of Spanish Succession, sails and makes purchase with Blackbeard, is known for being less vicious than most pirates, once captures a ship and boards, only to ask for the crewmen's hats, as his own crew had gotten drunk the night before and thrown theirs overboard—these gotten, he and his crew depart, leaving the vessel and its surprised crew in peace

bent bound and determined

'bent on a splice' about to be married [Gunner Jacobs seems bent on a splice, he do!]

berth a ship's home port, or, a ship's anchoring or mooring place

best bower the starboard bow anchor

'between the Devil an' the deep blue sea' the Devil is the seam in the deck planking closest to the side of the ship, if a sailor slips, he can find himself precariously between it and the deep blue sea [see the Devil to pay]

Beyond the Realms of Morning the place-name for the environs along the coast of Africa toward the yet-undiscovered Cape of Good Hope

Bible a block of sandstone used to scrub the deck [while on the knees, thus the name: compare to prayer book]

bight the rope, cable, or chain of an anchor

bilge the lowest point of a ship's inner hull, the angle of the hull between bottom and side, often carries one or two inches of water

bilge rat a pirate, sometimes used derogatorily, and perhaps not without humor, by other pirates, or, the actual animal living in the bilge

bilges the bottom compartment of a ship

bilge water collects in the bilges

billethead an often ornate structure just below the bowsprit to which is attached the figurehead

binnacle a housing for a ship's compass and its candle

bireme a Greek warship with two banks of oars

biscuit ship's bread, flat, hard dough-cakes [see hardtack]

Ye Olde Seafaring Lexicon

bitter end when all the anchor cable has been paid out [We've paid out to the bitter end, sir.]

bitts deck posts which ropes and cables are wound about to hold them fast

'Black Bart' never actually called this until the 20th Century, the teetotal, vicious, and rakish pirate Captain Bartholomew Roberts who took more plunder than any other known pirate— more than 400 ships in three years, originally forced aboard ship and made captain after the death of fellow Welshman Captain Davis, thought to have remained a pirate believing that if his ship was ever captured by the Royal Navy, he would be tried as a pirate even though he had been forced, would punish or kill his sailors if they didn't keep prayer hours

Blackbeard the mostly fictional pirate captain Edward Teach [Thatch] infamous for his greasy black beard adorned with lit fuses during action, his volatile temper, and his dozen or so wives, his flag is a black field emblazoned with the white skeleton of a horned demon holding a white hourglass and with a white spear jabbing [jobbing] a bleeding heart

Blackbeard's cup a legendary silver-plated goblet made from the feared captain's skull, its eye sockets forming part of the lip

blackbird any slave of Black African origin [Captain William Snelgrave commanded the slaver Bird Galley.]

Black Caesar's Clan a people allegedly yet living on Elliot Key, Florida and descended from the African-king-turned-pirate Black Caesar's harem, their ancestors are children of this harem who initially survived on berries and shellfish after Black Caesar left them to die, their mothers having already died of starvation

black cat if one comes aboard, especially uninvited, good luck prevails, if it is chased away, it takes the luck of the ship with it, the speaking of the word cat while at sea is unlucky [see cold iron]

Black Flag the pirate flag

Black Jack [1] the legitimate name for any black pirate flag, which has no one particular design but, more often than not, sports a black field and a white skull or skeleton, too commonly called the Jolly Roger

black jack [2] large drinking cups made of leather made stiffer with an application of tar

'black's the white o' me eye!' a sailor's resentful rebuttal of a charge of misdemeanor [Black's the white o' me eye, Cap'n, if I let the cat out o' the bag!]

black spot verbal or written mark of death [Theys put the black spot on ol' Cap'n Nate, sar, an' more's th' pity fer it!], too, a paper of deposing handed to a pirate captain seen to be 'fallin' slack in his dooty'

black strap any red wine

Black Squall a sudden squall of wind, accompanied by lightning, encountered in the West Indies

blaggard blackguard, pirate

blanket to aggressively cover another ship so that no wind can fill her sails

Bledmall a ferocious sea creature greatly feared by Irish and other Northern sea rovers, as it carries the uncanny ability to capsize the sturdy longships normally employed in coastal raids

'bleedin' the monkey' swigging grog in transit to mess [The Master caught Li'l Tim bleedin' the monkey yestreen. The cat'll be let out o' the bag tomorrow noon.]

'blimey!' an exclamation of surprise

block-and-tackle [blocks] ropes and pulleys used to raise heavy loads and increase purchase on ropes used for running rigging

Bloody Flag the red 'Flag of No Quarter' used mainly by pirates, but sometimes by the Navy and privateers, too, the large, square red flag hoisted by English warships to indicate they are going into battle

'blowin' great guns an' small arms' a heavy gale or hurricane [Laird, if it ain't gonna blow great guns an' small arms! Batten the hatches!]

'blow the grampus' waking a sailor asleep on watch by throwing a bucket of cold water on him

'blow me down!' an exclamatory note of surprise derived from the blowing of the wind in a gale

blunderbuss a short rifle with a flared muzzle, a common seaman's weapon

board [1] [above board] anything on or above open deck, something in plain view, honest [He's above board, sir, if there e'er wast an honest gentleman! I'd stake me life on it!]

board [2] to come alongside a ship in a boat or other small craft

boarding the preferred method of piratical engagement, reducing the chance of damaging the prize with gunfire, uncommon with most privateers, who prefer to destroy the enemy ship from a distance

boarding nets strung out from a ship's side to prevent boarding

boat hook a long pole with an iron hook on its end used for pushing or pulling boats

boatswain [bosun, botswain] literally, boat-boy, the officer in charge of the crew as well as sails, rigging, anchors, careening the hull and associated tasks

bobstays rigging extended between the cutwater and the bowsprit designed to hold the bowsprit down and steady [keep it from over-extending upward] as the ship bobs through choppy waters

Boctogaí faeries who abide in the sea, less friendly than land-faeries, thought to sport long yellow hair reaching to the middles of their backs, often 'mistaken for Mermaids [Sirens] or Merrows, but ostensibly of a different class of nature elemental

bole a ship's mast

boltrope a strong rope sewn to the edge of a sail to strengthen it

'bone o' whitewater curlin' in our teeth' i.e., We are sailing quickly and easily along, derived from the 'bone' of whitewater seemingly caught beneath the bow at the cutwater

Bonnet, Stede a colorful and pathetic man-of-letters-turned-pirate who begins a successful career, is invited into Blackbeard's ranks, is eventually browbeaten by the giant Teach and kept captive on his own ship, develops a grudge against the devilish ruffian after being allowed to depart from the latter's company, secures a letter of marque so as to pirate-hunt Teach, but instead turns back, perhaps in cowardice, to the easier life of piracy, for which he is subsequently captured and hanged until dead

Bonny, Anne sailed with Calico Jack, pardoned because she is found to be with child

booby house a 'house of ill repute'

boom a long spar used to extend the foot of a sail

bootleg to smuggle

booty the prize resulting from a purchase, loot

bore the battering ability of a cannon, the diameter of a cannon

bore up to push forward or advance

'born with a silver spoon in his mouth' said of any young gentleman able to enter the Navy without examination and with promotion assured

'born with a wooden ladle in his mouth' said of any seaman promoted by merit

Boston News Letter a newspaper of the early 18th century which routinely speaks of piratical activity along the coasts of the Americas

botswain's mate unknown on pirate ships, accords

often unwarranted discipline aboard Navy ships

bottled up to be cornered by enemy ships [We was bottled up fine when of a sudden Cap'n Swift maneuvered us out in such a fashion, all guns firing, 'twas of a sudden we wast before the wind and away quick as ye please.]

boucan [1] [French] wooden rack used by buccaneers upon which the meats of wild boar, oxen and other animals are smoked to then either be eaten, traded or sold, origination of a common pork delicacy

boucan [2] knife used by buccaneers when they hunt wild pig and oxen on the islands around Santa Domingo and Jamaica, come in all sizes and shapes and look like a cut-down cutlass, are primarily used as a utility knife, but can be used in combat to hack or slash an enemy in battle

boucan [3] bacon

bounty reward offered for the capture of a pirate

bounty hunter the captain out to capture a wanted pirate

bow [head] the extreme front of the ship

bowline a rope used to keep the weather edge of a square sail taut forward, attached to sails to pull them forward

bowshot a warning shot across the bow of a ship, demanding surrender

bowsprit [boltsprit] the heavy spar attached to the bow just above the billethead and carrying the jibboom and all headsails, rides just above the figurehead worn by larger vessels

box haul the sharp turning of a ship

brace [1] a rope used to control the horizontal movement of a square-sailed yard, used to hold the direction of a sail, enables the yard to be swung by a sailor on deck

brace [2] a pair, two, as in a brace of pistols

brace block a block at the end of a yard which a rope

passes through, enabling the yard to be swung by a person on deck

brace of pistols a set of two flintlock pistols more often than not tied to a silk sash which is then slung about the neck

brail a rope fastened to the leech of a sail and used for hauling the sail up or in

brailed up sails furled by tying them to the yard or mast

brass-bound man a Navy officer

brass monkey weather refers to very cold weather [see freezing the balls off a brass monkey]

breach the breaking of the sea into a ship, or over a coastal defense such as a seawall

break the gang to split piratical company, to each his own

bream to careen, to clean

breech a person's buttocks

Brethren of the Coast the original non-Spanish buccaneers of Hispaniola and later of Tortuga, 1640-1680

brick any projectile fired from a gun [cannon]

brig a re-rigged two-masted ship fully square-rigged on both masts, or square-rigged of the foremast and fore-and-aft rigged on the mainmast

brigantine [Spanish: brigantino: a brigands' ship] a small ship carrying both sails and oars, later a two-masted ship with foremast square-rigged and fore-and-afts on the main mast

Brigoméide [Welsh] a siren undine who loves all sailors and will save them if they are in distress, sometimes innocently insisting that in exchange they are obligated to come live with her beneath the depths [as she has never taken the time to see that humans cannot live for long underwater]

bring to [heave to] direct a ship into the wind so that it slows down and nearly stops

bring up to abruptly stop a ship, usually in an emergency and often with an anchor

briny deep the ocean

Bristol [Bristolman] a ship either manufactured in Bristol, England or departing from there

Britomartis [Cretan] the Cretan goddess of sailors, fishermen, and hunters

'broad in the beam' to have wide hips or buttocks, derives from the nautical term 'beam,' the widest point of a ship

broadside [1] the synchronized firing of all guns situated on one side of a vessel

broadside [2] to situate a ship starboard or port for a sea battle

broadsword often found with seamen from the Scottish Highlands, dispatched Blackbeard with a chop to his neck

broke his mind revealed his secret plans or the plans of a cabal or confederacy to [an alleged] sympathizer or sympathetic company [Carpenter Johnson broke his mind to us all last night, captain sir. It'd be a insurrection o' the most villainous variety!]

buccaneers [French: boucaniers] originally French, Dutch, and British adventurers joined by ship deserters, runaway servants, cimaroons and fugitives of all kinds [except the hated Spanish who sought to exterminate them] living on Hispaniola [Haiti] who slew and cured wild boar [bacon] and other animals there for eating, trade or sale, driven from the island by Spanish privateers, later set up a large encampment on the adjacent smaller but better fortified island of Tortuga and therefore, in revenge of their lost lifestyle, began in earnest all forms of piratical account against the Spanish Main, later relocated to Jamaica, Henry Morgan and Robert Searle [Robert Searles] are both classic buccaneers or Brethren of the Coast, sharply set apart from pirates or even corsairs by their intense hatred for the Spanish, the era of buccaneering lasted from 1640-1690

bucco [bucko] friend

bulkhead a vertical partition inside a ship often torn down by pirates to make room for stolen lading

bulwarks the vertical sides or walls of a ship below the main deck which pirates often pierce to make room for more guns

bumboat a small local boat which sells necessary items to ships at anchor

bumboo [West Africa] a drink of the West Indies made with watered rum and flavored with sugar and nutmeg

bumper a cup, pannikin, or glass filled to the rim and running over

bunghole the hole on the side of a barrel or cask through which the container is filled or emptied

bunt the middle part of a square sail, the part of a furled sail gathered up in a bunch at the center of a yard

bunting any flag or jack aboardship

buntline rigging used to hold or haul bunt

buoyed up when a buoy is used to raise the bight of an anchor chain so as to prevent it from abrasion on the seabed

burgoo ['American oatmeal'] boiled oatmeal porridge seasoned with salt, sugar, butter, and sometimes milk [if available]

'buried at Fiddler's Green' buried ashore

burth [berth] a place for the mooring of a ship

burthen [Middle English for burden] the carrying capacity of a ship, measured in tonnage

bury a vertical bulwark separating the ship's hull into two equal parts

busk to search for victims to attack

Ye Olde Seafaring Lexicon

butcher's bill the dead and wounded aboard after battle, often in the slaughterhouse

by and large by signifies to the wind, and large signifies with the wind, to sail by the wind signifies to sail into the wind as nearly as can be managed, to sail large signifies to sail with the wind blowing from astern, therefore, the phrase signifies that the ship [or anything else] is handled very well

'by guess an' by God' navigating without instruments

C

ca. [circa] about ['Cap'n Nort gave up the ghost circa 17 and 87, sar.']

cabal [Aramaic] to consort, plot secretively, probably from cabal or kabal, meaning 'hidden' and from which are derived the Spanish caballero and Hebrew kabala [Ye've been discovered caballin' with me men, ya dog! Ye'll be food fer fishes afore daybreak!], or, [n.] a secretive council concerning an intended purpose

cabin a room aboardship

cabin boy a young boy who works aboardship as a servant, many make their way aboard by being kidnapped by pirates or are runaways looking for a means of escape from their dismal way of life

cable a rope or chain used to raise or lower the anchor

caboose the galley or ship's kitchen

cackle fruit chicken eggs

cage [gibbet] an expensive metal framework made-to-order in which the tarred bodies of hanged or garroted pirates [usually infamous captains] are displayed, and often for many years, as anti-pirate propaganda

calfskins often used to make covers for cannon

calico any of several types of cotton cloth

Calico Jack the pirate John 'Jack' Rackam, who holds the four distinctions of wearing handmade clothes of calico, originally only pirating turtle and fishing boats, never having personally slain anyone, and having on his crew the two most famous female pirates Anne Bonny and Mary Read [who killed for him, among other duties they were apparently not averse to, both being saved from the gallows because of pregnancies when captured]

calms tranquil waters

canary wine of any vintage

candles allegedly, only two allowed to burn on any ship: one for the captain and one to read the compass by, thought punishable by death if caught burning after certain hours

caning [cobbing] punishment administered by Navy midshipmen to midshipmen in the privacy of the gunroom

canister shot a cylindrical tin or iron container made just smaller than the bore of the gun and containing a number of balls arranged round a central wooden core, used as an anti-personnel weapon, may too contain scrap metal

cannonade a cannon onslaught

canvas a sail

canvas jacket a protective coat worn at sea

cap large block of wood by which the base of an upper mast is fitted to the top of the next lower one

cape piece of land jutting into the sea

Cape, the Cape of Good Hope at the southernmost tip of Africa

Cape Horn the southernmost tip of South America

Cape Horn Fever the imaginary illness of sailors reluctant to go east to west round the treacherous Cape Horn

cap'n captain

capsize for a ship to heel over accidentally, as during a storm

capstan [windlass] a vertical cylinder upon which the ship's cable is turned

captain in piracy, a democratically elected leader who can be replaced at any time by a majority vote, or by mutiny, expected to be daring and clear-thinking, required to have consummate skills in the arts of navigation and deceit

captains' clothes worn by the pirate captain as a deceptive device to disguise himself as an admiral from afar, made up of breeches, a vest, a sea coat with tails, a lofty 'admiral's' hat with an ostrich feather or two, swashbuckler thigh-high boots, and even a pocket watch and fob [waistcoat, lace bunched at the throat, gold teeth, eye-patch, peg-leg, arm-hook, cummerbund, gold cross necklace and silk sash all optional or as needed]

caravel a small ship meant for trading, first lateen-rigged, later developed into a square-masted ship, ca. 80 ft. in length, carries a broad bow, a high poop, and triangular sails suspended from long diagonal arms

carbine a short rifle

carcass a ship-to-ship projectile made of an iron shell filled with saltpeter [potassium nitrate], sulphur, resin, turpentine, antimony [a metalloid constituent of alloys], and tallow, too outfitted with three holes for incendiary flames and pistol barrels which shoot randomly, creating much execution amongst men, thus its appellation

careen to heel a ship over in order to rid her hull of barnacles and seaweed [filth], to clean

Caribbean, the geographical map including the Caribbee Islands and Belize, Honduras, Nicaragua, Costa Rica, Panama and parts of Mexico, Colombia, Venezuela, Guyana and Florida, named after the Carib, a nation of American Indians of the Lesser Antilles and N. South America who shared their homeland with the Arawak and other Mesoamerican peoples

Caribbee Islands the isles of the West Indies [Caribbean Isles] mainly made up of Cuba, Hispaniola, Puerto Rico, the Bahamas, Jamaica, Trinidad, Tobago, Grenada, St. Lucia, Martinique, St. Vincent, Barbados, the Cayman Islands, Old

Ye Olde Seafaring Lexicon

Providence Island, St. Bartholomew Dominica, Guadeloupe, Tortuga, Antigua, Barbuda, Anguilla, St. Eustatius, Saba, St. Kitts, Nevis, Monserrat, the Leeward Islands, the Windward Islands, the Virgin Islands and several unnamed Carib strongholds

carouse [n.] a bout of heavy drinking often lasting several days, or even indefinitely, [v.] to enjoy such a bout

carpenter a highly skilled craftsman [mechanic or factor] responsible for maintenance and repair of all the ship's wooden parts, often a skilled cooper [barrel-maker], more often than not pressed or forced into service

carrack the largest ships before the advent of the galleon, often reaching 1,200 tons and used for trading voyages, three-masted with square sails on the fore and main masts and lateen-rigged on the mizzen, very high fore and aft-castles

Carras Dhoo [Manx] Manx pirates [Isle of Man] who lure ships to the rocky shores of Maughold Head

carronade a light cannon of large caliber used for short range

carry to capture a ship by laying her aboard and taking possession of her by means of a boarding party

cartel ship a ship employed in the exchange of prisoners

cartouche [French] a gun cartridge with a paper case

cartouche box an ammunition box holding cartridges or cannon balls

case-shot iron, stones, musket-bullets etc. put into a wooden [or woolen] case and shot from a cannon

castaway a shipwrecked sailor

Castellan the Spanish governor of a castle or keep

castle the superstructure fore and/or aft, of Medieval castle origin designed for fighting and built complete with wooden merlons and embrasures [the two parts of an actual stone castle's crenellated parapet {battlement} which create the classic checkerboard cut-out effect behind which soldiers hide and from which they shoot their arrows and bow-guns]

cat to raise the anchor from the water to the level of the forecastle [fok'sl]

Cathay the name by which China is known during the Mongol dynasty and thus in European nations during the early years of conquest in the 15th, 16th, and 17th centuries

cat-o'-nine-tails common punishment at sea, the actual instrument made, and often by the seaman to be punished, of braided and/or hemp cordage crafted in braid and/or macramé and making nine tails, each ending with a knot, the cat [He's let the cat out o' the bag now, he has.]

caul the mask on some newborn infants reputed, if kept safely or even worn around the neck, to protect the child from drowning his or her entire life, or to keep the entire ship from shipwreck if one happens to be aboard

caulk sealing the gaps between the planks with oakum and pitch, waterproofing

calavances small beans used for making soup

celestial navigation the method of using the north star or other constellations as reference points in navigation

centerboard a retractable keel

chains cordage extending from each mast and appended just below the rail at the uppermost part of the gunwale on both port and starboard, too known as mizzen-chains, main-chains, and fore-chains

chain-shot a round shot cut in two and reattached by a chain, used to bring down personnel, sails and rigging, too called angel-shot since there are no known cases of survival after its engagement with any sailor

chantey [shanty] a work song aboard ship or on the docks, short drag or short haul songs were for tasks requiring quick pulls over a relatively short time, such as shortening or unfurling sails, long drag or halyard songs were for heavier work requiring more setup time between pulls, for example, to get a heavy sail up to the mast, a song which gives the men a rest in between the hauls is what is required, the same song can too be used to lower the sails, this type of song usually with a chorus at the end of each line, used for long, heavy periods of labor and for long repetitive tasks, and need a sustained rhythm, raising or lowering the anchor while winding up the heavy anchor chain is their prime use [this winding is done by pushing round and round at the capstan bars, which requires a long and continuous effort], forecastle songs [forbitters] are sung in the evening, when the work is done, and it is time to relax, singing being a favored method of relaxation, songs sung can come from places visited, either at home or in some foreign land, naturally, songs of love, adventure, pathos, and famous men, battles, or just plain funny songs top the list, as far as whaling songs go, life on a whaler is worse than any other type of vessel, except maybe that of a pirate ship [in the sense of surviving]

chanteyman the sailor who assists work at the capstan and other stations of labor with his chant-like songs

chanteytown [shantytown] a small village in the outskirts of a town, or a quarter in town, where pirates and sailors gather, portions of the French Quarter [Vieux Carre] of New Orleans, or of the Spanish Quarter of Pensacola, Florida [before the arrival of white racist and imperialist Andrew Jackson] would be good examples

Charley Noble upon finding that the stack or stovepipe for the ship's galley was copper, merchant captain Charles Noble then required it to be kept polished, and so the stack took his name thereafter, old salts would kid around with the new recruit and tell him to find or summon 'Charlie Noble,' usually after much searching and being unable to find the person named, he will eventually discover that 'Charley Noble' is the stovepipe, this is akin to being put on lookout duty for the mail buoy, or being sent for the sky hook

Charlotte de Berry disguises herself as a man, joining the British Navy with her husband, eventually finds herself forced onto a ship to Africa, whose captain attacks her, leads a mutiny, beheads the captain, and turns the crew to piracy, raiding gold ships on the African coast, her pirate career demonstrates not only her own abilities, but too the thin line [or morally, no line] between then-legal imperialism and piracy, the gold she steals has originally been stolen from Africans, who are themselves being violently kidnapped by the slave trade—rapine of the worse possible kind, pirates such as she are taking what the Conquistadores have stolen from the Aztecs, Incas, and other peoples, her crew had been law-abiding sailors when serving under a sadistic rapist, but became outlaws when she led them

chase the ship being pursued [The chase be makin' full sail, sar!]

chase guns cannons at the bow employed when in pursuit of a ship

chasing shot a shot fired near the stern of a ship or onto one of her sides, demanding surrender

chearly quickly and/or heartily [Hoist high ol' Black

Ye Olde Seafaring Lexicon

Jack chearly, me messmate! We'll have us a purchase this day, b'God!]

cheer ship to cry out a cheer, usually of huzzahs, in honor of another ship

Cheng I Sao [Ching Shih] a lady pirate commanding an immense fleet, said to include between 1,500 and 1,800 ships and 80,000 pirates, in the China Sea in the early 19th century

chintz printed calico from India often taken as booty

chock-a-block when two blocks of rigging tackle are so hard together they can't be tightened further [Aye, we're chock-a-block, sure!]

Chocolate Gale the prevalent, brisk northwest wind of the West Indies and off the Spanish Main

Christopher Moody an 18th century pirate who holds a policy of no quarter, his flag is a red field, [then left to right] a yellow hourglass flying with black wings pointing up, a muscular white arm attacking with a dagger, a yellow skull with yellow crossed bones behind it

cimaroons [Spanish: cimmarones or cimmarons] runaway slaves who escape from the Spanish and lived in the mountainous and forested areas off the Caribbean, the pyrate Francis Drake, by some known as sir though he allegedly works for a living, often employs them to help him fight against their former masters

circumnavigate to sail completely around a point

clap aboard to capture or imprison by boarding an enemy ship

clap of thunder strong drink

clean [1] [bream] to clear weeds and barnacles from the bottom of a ship, careen

clean [2] to pillage

clean slate the slate upon which the watch-keeper records speeds, distances, headings and tacks, if there are no problems, the slate is wiped clean for the next watch, thus, to be allowed by the authorities to begin one's life of conduct over again

clew a metal loop attached to the lower corner of a sail, or, a lower corner, or only the after corner, of a sail

clewed cordage wound up into a ball, thus, by extension, wound up [The captain's clewed, Tom. I'd be wary as a hare in a wolf's hole if'n I wast ye.]

clewline the rigging running through the clew

close quarters close contact with the enemy

close with to do sea battle with

coaming a vertical rim surrounding hatch openings to keep any water on deck from entering below it, excellent for tripping over

coastguard any lighthouse keeper

cocked hat a bi- or tricorn hat, being a wide-brimmed hat turned up on two or three sides

cockra [West Indies] a wine made from palm nuts

coffin ship any slave ship

cog [German] a Medieval German merchant complete with castles fore and aft, and high beams making her difficult to board

cold iron touched as quickly as possible if a forbidden word has been spoken aboardship

colors a ship's flag

commodore the commander of a body of merchant ships

comb the cat to run the fingers through the tails of the cat-o'-nine so they don't stick together with blood and so cause permanent damage to the sailor being punished

come about turn round

'come clear off' to escape in a chase, if eventually caught by the pirates giving chase, in most cases no quarter is given and the captured crew is terribly used [tortured] if not killed outright for the trouble

'come into the measures' to agree to logical plans

Ye Olde Seafaring Lexicon

come smartly come quickly, as in coming about

come to anchor to lower or drop the anchor, the opposite of weigh anchor

commandeer to take a ship from her captain and crew, and either force them into service, enslave them, torture them for information and then kill them, disable their ship and leave them, or [on rare occasions, but not unknown] take only what is needed and let the crew go with their ship intact

commission when a government pays privateers to hunt down and attack an opposing country's merchant ships and return with its goods, nothing other than legalized piracy [Ye vessel 'Summer's Dooty' wast put under commission on the 20th inst.]

Commission of Reprisal during wartime, a commission allowing a privateer to take any enemy ship

commit to send one's ship in to attack another

company the crew

complement the number of seamen on a ship to form a complete crew, viz., a complement of 25, etc., pirate crews often have 100 or more men on a ship designed to be run by no more than 15-20

compliment cannon fire from an enemy ship

conquistadors [Spanish: conquistadoros] Spanish pirates concentrating on Mesoamerica

consigned ship a merchant allegedly heading for a foreign port but actually consigned to waiting pirates who show harmless violence as a ruse before taking her and capitalizing on the cargo

consort a vessel sailing in company with a pirate ship, often more heavily armed than the flagship

consortium a group of buyers going in together on a ship

consort ruse a trick used by pirate captains of only one ship where a pretend certificate of free passage is drawn up for the captain of a pilfered vessel so that, coming upon the pirate's imaginary heavily-armed consort, this unfortunate master can pass in safety, thus effectively keeping him from hailing the next legal ship and with them giving chase after the one pirate vessel

cook [ship's cook] often an ex-captain who has been lamed, partially blinded, or both, sometimes lazy and so hated by the crew

cooper a cask-maker, barrels [casks] being essential containers for water, food, supplies and various alcohols routinely consumed on the high seas, often a finished carpenter greatly coveted by pirates for his consummate skills

copper-bottomed genuine, trustworthy, as with a ship with this same physical quality

cordage rope, rigging

Cord Widderich a Dithmarsian taking revenge on his Frisian neighbors through piracy, in 1407, he and his men occupy Eiderstedt and make the Pellworm church tower their base for looting surrounding villages and deceiving ships into stranding, during his retreat from Pellworm, he carries away treasures, the most famous being a bronze baptismal font from the 13th century, settles in Büsum as a trader ca. 1412, and 35 years later, in 1447, is captured and hanged without trial.

corsair [Latin] a pirate of the Mediterranean Sea, but the name later employed by Caribbean pirates as a Romantic title for their profession

'corsairs parading crosses' a derogatory euphemism for the pirates known as the Knights of Malta, which are the reorganized Crusaders too known as Hospitaller Knights

'countenance all proceedings' to accept all trade, legal or illegal, look the other way, allow illegal activity in the name of good commerce [Be certain, Captain Shriek, that as governor of this fair colony I shall make it my most sincere duty to countenance all proceedings.]

country-ship a native ship of the waters in which it is sailing

course the charted route of a ship, and by extension, any obvious plans made or acts of Fate [Of course ye understand, sir, that me wife be heavy with child.]

coxwain [cox'n] the helmsman responsible for steering a rowed boat

cravat a neckcloth or scarf worn by seamen of all persuasions

Creoleans [French: too, Creoles] folk of primarily African slave situation or descent looked kindly upon by many pirates for their inability to defend themselves on the high seas, often become pirates of their own accord [without being pressed], occasionally seen by pirates as chattel slowing down a necessary departure, and so are left in burning ships

cross-dressing a piratical ruse to make an enemy think the ship is full of harmless women

crosstree yard

crowd after to give chase

crow's nest a coopered cut-barrel platform designed for lookout from the mainmast and/or other masts

cruiser an armed patrol ship

cruising to leeward searching the coast, usually for pirates

cut and run to cut the lashings on all sails and run away before the wind, regardless of direction, to cut the anchor cable and dispatch in quick escape

cutlass an inexpensive, slightly curved sword commonly used during piratical mêlée, the maritime blade of choice as it sports a sturdy hand-guard, is light yet strong, and can both chop and stab with equal efficiency

cut off wind to bear down or, by extension, to

strangle a person with the hands [He cut off Jim Paper's wind afore any could assist, sir.]

cut of the jib warships often cut down their triangular jib sails [fore-and-aft sails at the bow] so they can maintain point, merchants sighting narrowed jib sails may not like this and have time to escape a possible enemy ship, Ye can know a man by the cut o' his jib, or by the way his nose and face is shaped [phrenology, coined in 1805, is the word for the popular pseudo-science still in common use today when people say His eyes lay too close together or somesuch statement meant to define a personality]

'cut out a ship' [cut out of the road] to capture a lone ship, or a ship from her flotilla or fleet, often as specific revenge against the nation or company she represents

cutter a small, one-masted vessel rigged with fore-and-aft mainsail, foresail, and jib, usually has a square topsail, carries a complement of 15

cut the sail unfurl it and let it fall

cutwater the part of the bow of the ship, just above the forefoot, which slices through the water

D

dahabiah [Egyptian] a shallow-draft river vessel with high lateen sails

dalilah a prostitute, a bastardization of Delilah, the Philistine woman who played an important part in the deception of the Hebrew Judge Sampson, thus, a woman of ulterior motive and so, by wild extension, a woman of easy virtue [The rogues then took shore-leave to their dalilahs.]

'dance the hempen jig' to be hanged [Aye, Sam Girlish danced the hempen jig last e'en.]

'dance with Jack Ketch' to hang

Davey Jones a spirit of the sea deeply feared by many sailors, keeper of the dreaded locker where the souls of drowned sailors are imprisoned [i.e., Davey Jones' Locker, see soul cages]

davit a timber or iron crane projecting over the side of a ship used to hold small skiffs, anchors, or cargo

deadeye [dead-man's-eye] a large round block of wood carved with three holes for extending the shrouds, adopted as the symbol of the St. Photios Greek Orthodox Church shrine situated on the east side of St. George Street, north of Hypolita, in St. Augustine, Florida

deadeye rigging helps stay the foremast, its loop embracing the bowsprit

dead horse period of work already paid for while still in port [There's no sense in beatin' a dead horse!]

deadlights eyes [Engage yer deadlights, sirrah!]

'Dead men tell no tales' common excuse for leaving no survivors

dead reckoning deduced navigation noting compass

course, speed, elapsed time, drift from wind, and set
from current

dead water the eddy at the ship's stern

death's head the ink sketch used originally to denote
the death of a seaman in the captain's log, allegedly
appropriated by pirates for the Jolly Roger

'declare war against all the world' the typical
piratical disposition, i.e., 'the world owes me a
living'

deep six to discard something, specifically to throw it
in the water, water depth is measured in fathoms,
six feet to a fathom, this term comes from the
throwing of the lead to determine water depth and
indicates a depth 'over six fathoms'

demijohns large bottles of earthenware or glass with
narrow necks and wicker casing and handle[s]

depose to democratically vote a pirate captain out of
office by handing him the 'black spot', a piece of
paper with the word 'deposed' or some other term of
dismissal written on it

derelict any vessel abandoned at sea

desperadoes [Spanish: from desperados] pirates

devil the hard-to-get-at seam at the side of the ship,
too, the seam at the waterline

dhow meant to be a trading ship with a single mast
lateen-rigged, 150 to 200 tons, Arab pirates favor
this ship after arming it with cannon

'didn't know what was comin' off' an after-the-
fact statement concerning a quick event leading to a
bumfuzzlement, a disaster, or a death, taken from
the all-too-common occurrence of ship's cordage
and other equipment coming loose above and falling
to deck, i.e., I didn't know what was happenin' ta me
or He didn't know what hit him

'die like a soldier' to be shot instead of hanged

dinner the noon meal of bread and beer with beef or
pork four out of seven days and cheese and oatmeal

the remaining days, desserts include figgy-dowdy
and, for officers, plum duff or spotted dog

Dinney Mara the ocean spirit whose name means
'Man of the Sea', to whistle aboardship is to cause
him to bring more wind than is required to sail a
ship, therefore that form of musical entertainment is
prohibited by all except the captain and his officers

dirk a short sword worn by Scottish Highlanders and
common among seamen

discover to inform on piratical plot, activity, etc.

'discover no fondness for' to dislike an idea,
person, etc. [I soon discovered no fondness for Red
James.]

disembogue [French] to go out at the mouth of a
gulf

dispatch [1] to sail out or away onto an unknown
course

dispatch [2] to kill somebody

distribution of justice a common practice of
pirates questioning Navy or merchant sailors as to
whether they are being treated fairly or no, in hopes
that the crew will join their own endeavor [without
being pressed, which causes unnecessary and often
fatal problems in future]

ditty box a wooden box in which letters from home
are kept

dog a sailor, especially any pirate

dog biscuits hardtack, ship's biscuits, sea biscuits

Dog Days early July through early September in the
Western Hemisphere when the weather becomes
sultry and unbearable, and malaria is at its worst

doit [Dutch] a Dutch coin equal to one-eighth stiver

dog watch the two half-watches of two hours each
into which the period from 4 to 8 post meridian is
divided, the purpose of dividing this watch into two
is to produce an uneven number of watches in the
24 hours, seven instead of six, thereby ensuring that

watchkeepers in ships, whether organized in two or three watches, do not keep the same watches every day, these two watches are known as the First Dog and Last Dog

Doldrums the belt of calm which lies inside the trade winds of the northern and southern hemisphere, this area, which lies close to the equator, has great significance as the trade of the world is carried by sailing ships, the areas immediately north and south of the trade winds too used to be known as this, by extension, mentally depressed [Ach, I'm in the doldrums again, boyo, an' canna figger why.]

dolphin striker a boom jutting downward from the bowsprit to which are attached stays for the headsails, too, the martingale

dory a flat-bottomed boat used for fishing

double cannon ball two cannon balls linked by an iron bar, used to bring down sails and rigging in a similar fashion as angel-shot

doubloon [Spanish] a gold coin made of metal mined by the enslaved Indians of Mexico, Bolivia, and Peru, worth at various times between 4 to 16 pesos

'down by the head' malformed, said of both ships and pirates [I say it lowly, sir, for fear of reprisal, but this crew is down by the head, and make no mistake.]

Down East along the coast of Maine

'down helm!' the command to spin the wheel around port or starboard [Down helm port!]

draft the depth of water a ship draws when loaded

drag a kind of floating anchor, usually made of spars and sails, used to keep a ships head to the wind or to diminish leeway

Drake, Francis an English knighted slaver, pyrate, and Elizabethan Sea Dog

draw, the how deep into the water a ship sinks

Ye Olde Seafaring Lexicon

'dressed to the nines' all 'nine yards' or three masts of a ship-of-the-line dressed in celebratory bunting, flags, colors, etc.

dressing down [1] treating old or worn sails with oil or wax to refurbish them

dressing down [2] a severe reprimand in the hopes of salvaging a Navy seaman

drift the distance the wind has taken a ship

drive to move driven from anchor in a storm [Does the ship drive, sir?]

drive ashore to sail a small ship onto a sandy beach to port

drivelswigger one who reads about nautical and piratical terms to an extreme, an 'armchair sailor'

'driven from anchor' when a storm moves a ship into deep sea though she is anchored

drogher [West Indian] a West Indian coasting vessel with long, light masts and triangular sails

drogues [French] a ruse de guerre of improvised implements tied to cordage and dragged behind a ship to keep her from sailing too fast, thus seeming to be a heavily-laden merchant

dromon a form of Greek merchantman propelled by oars or sail

drop back to slow up to join another ship

drub to beat or thrash with a stick or a naked cutlass

dugout a canoe made of a tree trunk which has been carved out, common in the Caribbean

'duly brought to the chest' the Navy tradition of whipping seamen with a rod every Monday morning as they lay over, tied, to the gunner's daughter, believed to ensure proper winds for sailing

dungbie rear end

Duppy Jonah the origination of the appellation Davy Jones, literally from both the West Indies and Biblical allusion, 'Demon of Sea Misfortune'

Dutch East India Company an unscrupulous

merchant company from Holland whose counterpart is the English East India Company

'Dutchman's breeches' [sailor's trousers] two patches of blue appearing in a stormy sky giving promise of better weather, enough blue sky to make a pair of breeches

Dutchman's log a rough method for finding a ship's speed by throwing a piece of wood into the sea well forward and timing its passage between two marks on the vessel known a distance apart

edging forward refers to slow advance by means of repeated small tacking movements, origin of 'get a word in edgewise'[No sar, couldn't get a word in edgewise with the rapscallion!]

Edward England a very lenient and thus marooned pirate captain, his flag is made up of a black field with a white skull and crossbones, the bones crossed aneath the chin, considered the classic pirate flag because, for whatever reason, it is the one most widely recognized, though the original Jolly Roger is most probably the Flag of No Quarter sporting only a plain red field

Edward 'Ned' Low a flagitious pirate captain born in Westminster and raised as a pickpocket and housebreak on the streets of London, after the heartbreaking loss of his wife and infant son, he made the statement upon coming on a sloop that he and his gang would 'go in her, make a black flag and declare war against all the world,' this he did, and once during his career he burned a French cook alive, saying he was a 'greasy fellow who would fry well,' at another instance he slew 53 Spanish captives with his cutlass, he was later either lost in a storm or hanged by the French, his flag is a black field with the figure of Death in red

effective occupation the Spanish act of occupying land in the Caribbean before Dutch, English, and French conquerors arrive

Eight-Year Terror the years 1714-1722 when piracy is at its most horrendous apex

El Castillo de San Marcos [Spanish: constructed 1672-1695] the heavily fortified fort on the Matanzas River bayfront in St. Augustine, Florida built by slaves in response to the massacre led by pirate captain Robert Searle [aka Robert Searles] in May 1668

El Draque [Spanish] The Dragon, the Spanish name for the feared English pyrate Francis Drake

elephants' teeth ivory from any source, prized for its great trade value

embroidery a popular pastime among mariners at sea

emperor a large-scale pirate captain

emulation ambitious or envious rivalry said of two ships, a company of pirates, etc.

endure put up with [I'll ne'er endure a Virginiaman again, lest no quarter be giv'n to the dogs!]

engaged at battle

English East India Company an unprincipled trading company and the main rival of the Dutch East India Company

ensign a military flag or banner

ensign staff the flagstaff for the ship's national flag [ensign] or colors of ruse de guerre

Equatorial Current the ocean current used by most European sailors to enter the Caribbean

escopette [French] a flintlock musket

Eustace the Monk a Flemish monk-turned-pirate executed by the Norman-English in the year 1217

even keel floating upright in the water without list, said of unexcitable sailors and officers [He's always on even keel, mate. Not to worry.]

Execution Dock, at Wapping on the north bank of the River Thames in London where perpetrators are staked down at low tide and allowed to slowly drown, in later days they are hanged, tarred and then, if renowned, placed in gibbets to slowly rot [Aye, he steered his course t'ward Execution Dock, he did, an' more's the pity fer it!]

Ye Olde Seafaring Lexicon

Exquemelin, Alexander Oliver pirate author of
The Buccaneers of America [first published in 1678]
after he served with the buccaneers under Henry
Morgan from 1666-1674

F

faggot a Navy seaman secretly paid off to answer for an absent man at muster

fair wind any favorable wind, by extension, good luck! [Godspeed, and a fair wind to ye, mate!]

falcon a small cannon which fires a 3-pound ball

'fall by the board' usually having to do with something breaking or falling from above, as a mast cracking while under full sail, by extension, the downward spiral of any sailor [John Nott soon fell by the board and went on piratical account.]

fall down to have a mishap with a ship, such as running aground in shallow water

'fall in with' to come upon to plunder [or fight, as the case may present itself], too, to join company with other ne'er-do-wells [Lacy Jacobs fell in with the rakehells, and soon became their captain.]

'fall together by the ears' for a company to have it out with one another, usually violently [And as they fell together by the ears, I made my escape along the coast.]

Farmagud [Scandinavian] the god of Nordic seafarers

fathom six feet

fathom out to ascertain a water depth, thus, to deduce something

fearnought a short woolen coat worn in port, made of heavy blue or grey material, worn at sea if waterproofed with tar or wax

felucca [Arabic] a fast, narrow lateen-rigged vessel found chiefly in the Mediterranean Sea

fence to purchase and resell [at a higher price] goods brought to port

fend off bearing a vessel off with spar or boathook to

avoid violent contact when coming alongside

fetch to raise or come to an anticipated or hoped-for cape or landmass [We fetched Hispaniola on the 13th inst.]

field piece a mobile cannon

fid similar to a marlinspike, but larger and made of wood; used in the same way as a marlinspike but usually for larger rope and cable

Fiddler's Green a happy port where old sailors go if they don't go to Hell

figgy-dowdy crumbled hardtack mixed with lard [pork fat], plums, currants [Corinths], and rum

figurehead a wooden carving, usually of a voluptuous woman, attached just below the bowsprit

filth accumulation on a ship's hull made of barnacles, seaweed, etc. [We careened for the purpose of burning off our mass of filth, so long had we been at good account in those rich waters.]

fireship ship set afire and sailed toward the anchored enemy, in this way the English pyrate Francis Drake defeated the ill-fated Spanish Armada

first mate serves as apprentice to the boatswain, carpenter, and gunner, takes care of the outfitting of the vessel to see that enough ropes, pulleys, deadeyes, sails, and all other rigs are available for a voyage, hoists or weighs anchor and checks the tackle once a day, anything awry is reported, in port, he causes the cables and anchors to be repaired, and manages the sails, yards, and mooring of the ship

fish a plank of wood bound around the mast to strengthen it

fisherman's anchor the classic sailing anchor looking much like a double fish hook

'fish food' a dead sailor

fit out to outfit a ship for voyage, provision her

fit up to change a ship's appearance, usually via carpentry, to the specifications of the commandeering pirate captain

flagitious heinous, monstrous, atrocious, often said of pirates

flagship a pirate captain's own ship in his fleet of various craft, or, a ship commanded by a Navy admiral

flaw a sudden gust of wind

flintlock the common pistol used by seamen, Blackbeard carries 3 brace of these [6 guns in total]

flip a nautical drink consisting of hot small beer and brandy, sweetened and spiced upon occasion, according to one description of Henry Avery, he took holiday 'at Madagascar with some drunken sunburnt whore, over a can of flip.'

flog to punish with the cat-o'-nine-tails

'flogged round the fleet' the punishment when a sailor is rowed round to every ship in the harbor fleet and flogged

'flogging a dead horse' [beating a dead horse] to vainly expect more work out of seamen while they are working off a dead horse, i.e., Give up, it's useless

flood-tide a rising or incoming tide as opposed to an ebb tide, excellent for going ashore

flota [Spanish] treasure fleet

flotilla [Spanish] battle fleet

flotsam floating remnants of a shipwreck or exploded vessel

'flotsam and jetsam' derogatory appellation for a crew of pirates

flush deck a deck re-crafted by the ship's carpenter so as to provide needed room for the extraordinary number of pirate crewmen [see complement], and for skirmish when boarded, the quarterdeck and foredeck are made flush with the main deck of the ship, or, a deck naturally crafted with no elevated decks

Ye Olde Seafaring Lexicon

'fly at high game' busking with probability of great purchase

fly-boat [Dutch: flute] large flat-bottomed Dutch vessel of 400 to 600 tons burthen, distinguished by a remarkably high stern which resembles a Gothic turret, and by very broad buttocks below, noted for her cargo-carrying capacity

fly-by-night a large sail used only for sailing downwind and requiring little attention

following sea high water threatening the stern of a ship [Ah, she's a following sea this night.]

footloose the unsecured bottom portion of a sail

footrope [1] the rope rigged below a yard for men to stand on

footrope [2] a part of a boltrope sewn to the lower edge of a sail

forbidden words causing ill luck aboardship, viz., church, chapel, manse, cat, eggs, or minister

forbitters chanteys sung round the forecastle telling of past victories and glories, in contrast to work chanties

force [1] the act of making an unwilling seaman sign the pirate articles of a ship upon fear of death, forced men usually have a special skill or knowledge the pirates need, and include surgeons, navigators, carpenters, blacksmiths, and musicians [who, on many ships, are made to play every day except Sunday, and during all fights, regardless of day]

force [2] to rape a woman, a common [and often communal] piratical practice normally ending in the dispatching of the unfortunate creature, commonly via snapping her spine and making her fish food

fore situated at the front of a ship

fore-and-aft at bow and stern, or along the length of the craft

fore-and-aft rig mainly fore-and-aft sails, which are sails set lengthwise and not at right angles to the hull

forecastle [pronounced and even spelled fok'sl] the castle behind the bow

forefoot the portion of the ship just below the cutwater

foremast the front mast

foremastmen ordinary seamen so called because their quarters are before the foremast

foresail the first or primary sail on the foremast from the deck

fore-scuttle the forward hatchway or opening in the deck

fore-topgallant yard the yard holding the topgallant sail

foretopmast the mast above the foremast

fore-topsail the sail on the foremast above the foresail, or, the second sail in ascending order from the deck on the ship's forward mast

fore-topsail halyards vertical ropes for hoisting the sail above the foresail on the foremast

forge over to move over a shoal or sandbar with wind power

form station to flank a ship well astern in her honor

fothering temporarily stopping a ship's leaks by using the pressure of the sucking action to hold a piece of canvas or to suck in pieces of rope-yarn let down into the water in a basket

foul [1] wrong or difficult ['Twas was a foul port, and we weighed anchor with a quickness.]

foul [2] [filth] when a ship is covered with barnacles, seaweed, etc.

founder when a ship's deck sinks below the surface of the water [An' when she foundered, we prayed to Davy for safe passage.]

four-pounder the typical gun size on a pirate sloop, fires a roundshot circa 1,000 yards [3,000 feet]

freebooter pirate

Ye Olde Seafaring Lexicon

'freezing the balls off a brass monkey' a brass monkey is a brass triangle which is put on the ground and used to keep cannonballs in a neat pile or pyramid beside a gun, when the weather gets very cold the brass triangle contracts more than the iron balls and so causes the cannonballs to roll off, hence the saying

French filibusters [Dutch: vrijbuiter, or freebooter] buccaneers originally from Hispaniola, their flag a black field with white bones crossed behind a white skull, a white hourglass centered beneath [this being too the Emanuel Wynn banner]

frigate to the Venetians [Venetian frigate], a small oared boat ca. 35 feet in length and 7 feet wide, to the British, a large ship which carries oars, circa 1700, the British limit the name to mean a class of warship only second in size to the first-rate ship-of-the-line, three-masted with raised forecastle and quarterdeck, from 24 to 38 guns on her deck, faster than man-o-wars and used for escort purposes, sometimes used to hunt pirates, who normally flee from this vessel and therefore rarely commandeer one

'from the sea' when answering a hail as to what country pirates claim allegiance, they answer 'From the sea,' as they are loyal to none except themselves

frontal of cord [woolding] a torture where a cord of leather or rope is wrenched tighter and tighter round the head with a bar or stick until the eyes of the victim pop out, if twisted tighter, the skull cracks and the brains of the unfortunate fly loose

full blown when the sails are fully filled with wind, by extension, all the way, or the best job possible

full sail ahead all sails unfurled in chase or venture in open sea

full to the gunwales packed to the sides of the ship

furies pirates often called this, meaning demons

Ye Olde Seafaring Lexicon

furl to roll up sails or colors
fusil [Latin] a light flintlock musket
fuste [Spanish: fusta] a favorite vessel of Barbary
  corsairs, small with both sails and oars, fast, long
  and low in profile
futtock shrouds pieces joining the rigging of lower
  and top masts

G

gaff [see gaff-topsail] the spar on which the head of a fore-and-aft sail is extended

gaff-topsail a triangular sail set above the gaff

gale a freezing hurricane-force wind common in the North Atlantic

galeota [Dutch or Flemish] galliot, galiot

gallant roguery the condition of mind where the pirate captain and crew are always ready to fight and die if need be, but never turn coward and strike colors

galleas [Latin] similar to a galley, but with broadside guns and oars, has less firepower than a galleon, but can move even if there is no wind

galled extremely angry, put out, often unto revenge [With his last words the master galled me.]

galleon [Spanish] a three-masted ship with 2 to 3 decks and heavily armed with three or four batteries of cannon, meant for transporting cargo, unable to sail into or near the wind, two to three decks, the forward mast is square-rigged, the mizzenmast is lateen-sailed, and the bowsprit carries a small square sail, this ship can carry 4 masts, but this is unusual

galley [1] 13th century flat-built warship with one naturally flushed deck and powered by oar and sail, Captain Kidd made his name in his Adventure Galley

galley [2] the kitchen of any ship

galley stores a ship's rations of salted meat, hardtack [ship's biscuits] and other bare essentials for survival

galliot [Dutch or Flemish: galiot, galeota] 14th century variant of the galley used primarily by

Barbary pirates and corsairs [Mediterranean pirates] but too by pirates in the New World of the 16th-18th centuries, a long, sleek, single-mast double lateen-sail vessel [two vertical spars] and 6-12 oars each side, a naturally flushed deck [as opposed to a vessel made flush by the ship's carpenter after a commandeering], carries from 2 to 10 small cannon, powered by both wind and oar and can hold as many as 50-130 men, when lawful, usually employed in coastal trade

gallivat a large boat [small ship] with both sails and oars and mounting 4 to 8 swivel guns, of 40 to 70 tons burthen, carrying ca. 100 men for landing, rowed with 30-40 oars, holds ca. 20 fighting men besides the rowers, or, a boat similar to the fast felucca, from which comes the phrase gallivating around

gambling and dicing expressly forbidden on all Navy ships and many pirate vessels, but enjoyed nonetheless, though clandestinely

gang a pirate company [crew, parcel, etc.]

'gangway!' a command to get out of the way

garble the prohibited yet apparently common act of mixing garbage with the cargo, and then selling all as good cargo

garrote [Spanish] an alternate to hanging where the victim is manually strangled to death with a rope, the preferred method of the Spanish

gasket a line or band used to lash a furled sail

Gate of Tears the passage into the Red Sea, named by Arab sailors for the many shipwrecks there

'Gatos muertos no dicen meu' [Spanish: Dead cats don't meow] Dead men tell no tales

gear ropes, cordage, block-and-tackle

Genthus of Illyria pirate of the ancient world, sailed the Mediterranean ca. 181 BCE., was accused by the Romans of organizing and aiding pirate raids in

Ye Olde Seafaring Lexicon

Italy

gentle heel the coveted soft rocking of the ship making it easier to read the astrolabe, embroidery, carve scrimshaw, etc.

gentlemen of fortune pirates

gentry, the pirates

get clear stand off to fight

getting under way heading out on course

ghost to make headway with no apparent wind

ghost-sentry a pirate chosen by short straw and then slain by his mates at the site of buried treasure so as to haunt away anyone later thieving it [see Who'll go?]

gibbet [1] the gallows where hanging [or garroting] until then dead takes place

gibbet [2] the expensive cage hanged bodies of renowned pirates are displayed in

'give actions a color' to seek to make illegal actions appear legal, or, to rationalize piratical action

give over an engagement when a lesser ship on the more harmonious side of the law ceases fire and leaves a pirate ship it has engaged

give over chase to cease a chase, often because the chased ship is faster

give wide berth to keep ships from hitting one another when they swing with the wind or tide

glass [1] a telescope

glass [2] an hour-glass [sand-glass]

go about the command to turn the ship back

go a-cruizing [1] [go a-pirating] when pirates go in search of piratical account

go a-cruizing [2] when lawful seamen go on account

go by the board to throw overboard, thus, to be finished with ['He'll go by the board, he will, he keeps it up, lad.']

godspeed speed of the gods, by extension, good luck and safe voyage

gold earrings worn by Navy seamen to insure proper burial at home, worn by pirates as jewelry, but helps pay for their hangings, garrotes, unmarked graves, or cages [gibbets]; commonly believed to keep sailors from being drowned

Golden Age of Piracy, the 1690 through 1725-30

'go off halfcocked' when a musket or pistol is half-cocked and goes off anyway, thus, to act irrationally and dangerously, or to act unprepared [No need to go off halfcocked, Pip Dooley.]

'go on account' become a pirate

grab [Dutch: grabb] Dutch East India Company-built 150 ton three-masted cargo vessel with a prow like a row-galley instead of a boltsprit, officered and armed like a man-o-war

Grace O'Malley [Irish: Granuaile Ní Mháille] a Connaught, Ireland clan chieftain of the 16th century who is too captain of 27 viking and pirating vessels, considered one of the female personifications of Ireland, the only daughter of sea captain and clan chieftain Dudara [Black Oak] O'Malley, and Margaret O'Malley, a noblewoman from another branch of the clan

grandee [French] an aristocrat or high official on a voyage who is exempt from all labor

grapeshot anti-personnel shot made of iron balls the size of grapes and often used in broadside attack

grappling hook an essential boarding tool

grave the ship to bring her to lie aground, to burn off her old filth [barnacles, seaweed 'beards,' etc.]

Greater Antilles the islands of the Caribbean to include Cuba, Hispaniola, Jamaica, and Puerto Rico

Great Gun Salute the firing of the great guns wide or into the air as a custom when pirates meet one another

Great South Sea renamed the Pacific Ocean

Greek fire naphtha [any hydrocarbon petroleum

solvent], sulphur, and pitch [pine tar] ignited and thrown at sails, cordage, and personnel

Greekly cunning

grenadoe [Spanish] grenade, a common pirate weapon consisting of a square-faced case bottle containing gunpowder, small shot, and pieces of scrap iron

grinning a popular face-pulling competition wherein a horse collar is put around the neck of the competitor to frame his hideous expression, prizes are awarded to the winner, a similar occupation is employed, in the attempt to scare sharks away from the ship, where the sailor has ropes tied to his ankles and then is let down to make scary faces at the animals

groat a British coin worth four pennies

grog a rum drink of three to four parts water to one rum, brown sugar [cane sugar crystals filmed with refined dark syrup] and lemon or lime juice, commonly found on ships, but only after 1740 [some say 1731] when it is created by Admiral Vernon [Old Grogram] to help cure his sailors of scurvy

groggy the result of drinking too much grog, or, by extension, foggy from too little or too much sleep

grogram boat cloak a coarse silk cloth cloak often mixed with mohair or wool and stiffened with glue, worn by Admiral Vernon [called Old Grogram] who created grog for his men's health

grometta [Spanish] servant

ground to disable a ship by hitting a shoal or, worse, rocks or reefs

ground tackle cable and anchors, and equipment used to lift them

grub food

gruel a hot, watery cereal made from corn meal and given to the infirm

Guarda-Costa [Spanish: Guarda del costa] the

Spanish coastguard in the West Indies routinely resorting to piratical endeavor, the French version being the Guard de la Coste

guerre de course [French] privateering

Guineyman [Guineaman] a large, 26-gun Dutch-built French merchant built for trade with the Guinea coast of Africa

gulden [Dutch] the Dutch coin equal to 100 cents

Gulf of Mexico the highly pirated waters with such ports as Vera Cruz, San Juan de Ullua, Mobile [Alabama], and Pensacola [Florida], these latter two cities named after American Indian tribes routinely warring with one another, viz., the Mobila and the Panzacola

gun specifically, a cannon, the last-resort weapon of most pirates for fear of damaging the potential prize, often used to fire a surrender shot across the bow or toward the stern or sides of a victim vessel

gunner by necessity, almost any sailor aboard

gunner's daughter the gun to which Navy sailors are tied every Monday morning to receive their requisite whippings

gunports built into pierced hulls

gunwale pronounced 'gunnels', the planking below the rail along the sides of a craft from which deck cannon protrude

gybing veering in a fore-and-aft rigged vessel

Gypsy lantern a makeshift candle-lantern made of a wine bottle with its base broken out by inserting many nails, points down, and shaking

hail to call to another ship to know where she is bound, or from whence she comes

hail in to come into shore for security [We'll hail in this night, messmates.]

half-crown a British silver coin worth two shillings and sixpence

hall hide [The Deplorable halled into a lagoon, and so was lost by the Guarda-Costa.]

halter the hangman's noose

halyards vertical ropes for hoisting sails

hand-over-fist quickly and continuous, as with hauling cordage

hands sailors

handsomely the command to ease off the line, or tackle, carefully and gradually [Handsomely, now!]

handspike [handspeak] a kind of lever or crowbar, usually made of wood and often used as a weapon

hand-to-hand the pirate's preferred way of battle with another ship so that the prize is not damaged

hang the jib frown [There's no need to be hangin' the jib, Tom Funk.]

hanged at the yardarm the common punishment for apprehended Navy mutineers and single seamen who have willingly become pirates

hanged, drawn, and quartered a slow-death torture where the victim is first swung by the neck until nearly dead, then has his intestines drawn out, and then is beheaded and quartered, each body part often sent to an area where insurgent friends of his abide, the head is invariably spiked and displayed

hanged out of the way hanged [so as to be out of the way of society]

hanging fire when a musket or flintlock pistol fails

to fire its ball but the fire is still present, and so the
bullet can go off at any time, thus, bad blood or ill
feelings toward one or more persons

hard and fast **a** ship firmly beached on shore, thus,
without doubt or debate [Captain's word be hard
and fast, mate. Get used to it.]

hardtack a resilient, tasteless, unleavened bread
made of flour and water and not prone to
corruption, a hard type of water-biscuit made for
long sea voyages, four inches square and a quarter
inch thick, dog biscuits, sea biscuits

hard up in a clinch and no knife to cut the seizing,
desperate

harquebus [French] a small caliber long-gun with a
matchlock or wheel-lock mechanism

hat feathers stolen and only worn for piratical
action

hatch a horizontal door on deck leading below

haul pirate booty

haul a sail done with clewline and buntline

haul off to move away from land or another ship

haul up! heave sail and rigging in a lively manner

haul wind to direct course as near as possible to the
direction from which the wind is coming

have a care of the lee latch go not too much the
leeward, and so by extension, be careful [Have a
care o' the lee latch, lad. The crew'll not take kindly
to yer chatter.]

have the Davies [or the Joneseys] to be frightened

have the heels to be safely ahead while being chased

hawse part of the ship's bow containing the
hawseholes, or holes in the bow through which
cables pass

hawser a large rope for towing, mooring, or securing
a ship

head, the bow, too, the place where the sailor both
urinates and defecates by hanging his breech out

over the bowsprit and holding on for dear life

head attire common are scarves, tricorn or slouch hats, and woolen Monmouth caps or montero caps

headsails the sails extending from the bowsprit and jibboom, or, any sail forward of the foremast

headway motion in a forward direction [Aye, we've good headway now, lads!]

head winds blowing in the direction opposite to the ship's course or straight at the bow

heartie affectionate name for a sailor [Drink up, me heartie! Down the hatch!]

heave down to heel a craft over

heave to [bring to] a command to check or stop the course of a ship by laying her on the wind with her helm a-lee and sails shortened and so trimmed that as she comes up to wind she falls off again on the same tack and thus makes no headway, to bring her to a standstill by heading her into the wind

hector [derived from Hector, the name of the accidental enemy of the pirate Achilles] any bully, often said of pirate captains and other crew members

heel [1] to either accidentally or intentionally turn a ship over, the latter for careening

heel [2] to dangerously have the ship lay over to one side or the other while she is sailing

helm the wheel [tiller] controlling the rudder and steering the vessel

helmsman the sailor in charge if the wheel [rudder]

hemp ship's cordage made of the fibers of the plant Cannabis sativa

hempen halter hangman's noose, made of hemp rope

Hendrick Jacobszoon Lucifer Dutch pirate of the early 17th century who uses fire and smoke as his primary battle tactic, thus his nickname serving as surname

heterosexuality an act engaged in freely while at port, with syphilis and gonorrhea cases rising rapidly once the ship is again at sea

'He walks on his heels' [He does well with his money] based on the common superstition that the wear of the sole of the shoe determines how a man uses his money, if he walks on his toes, for example, he is a profligate, spendthrift, or wastrel

Henry Avery [Every] a pirate whose aliases included John Avary, Long Ben, and Benjamin Bridgeman, is most known for being one of the few major pirate captains to retire with his loot without being arrested or killed in battle

high and dry stranded, without help or hope of recovery

high seas the waters far away from land

high seas larceny piracy

highwayman [cutthroat] land pirate

His Majesty's Pardon [the King's Pardon] an open pardon signed on the 5th of September 1717 by King George I and granted by British colonial governors to British pirates tired of running the hazard of the neck, usually asked for after a particularly pleasurable purchase

hitch any of the various common rope knots and ties used aboard ship to include splices, figure-8 knots, sheepshanks, bowlines, reef knots, and clove hitches

Ho! used to attract attention to something specific [Land, ho! or Ho! Lively there!]

hoa, hoa! the common call to another ship

hogshead a large cask or barrel used for dry or liquid goods, holds between 63 and 140 gallons

hoist to raise colors or sails

hold a ship's cargo compartment

Holland a coveted fine linen, often speckled, manufactured in Holland

Holland shirt a shirt made of Holland

Ye Olde Seafaring Lexicon

Hollow of the Sea [Trough of the Sea] the particular phenomenon where the sea opens up deeply and sends the head or stern of a ship down into its maw; maelstrom

holystone bars of sandstone used to scrub the decks, the softer areas of the stone wearing away and leaving holes, too, sailors are said to look as if they are praying as they kneel to scrub

homosexuality punishable by death on both sides of the law, but not entirely unknown aboard ship and elsewhere

honorably discharged when captives are let go, often with a new set of clothes

honor of the day, the more powerful ship

hornpipe a three-in-measure Celtic dance changed to a two-in-measure dance popular with seamen

hornswoggle cheat, gyp [derogatory to Gypsies], Jew down [derogatory to those of Judaic background]

Horse Latitudes waters with strange weather patterns between the south-western coast of Africa and South America

hostis humanis generis [Latin: hostile to all humanity] said of pirates

hot roaring drunk, and so courageous for all manner of piratical account

hot shot [red hot shot] shore battery [and sometimes aboard ship] round shot heated for aim at a ship's sails and pitched deck, shot heaters may be seen, among other places, at El Castillo de San Marcos in St. Augustine, Florida

hove [1] to turn a vessel onto her side for cleaning

hove [2] came [As Lady Luck would have it, a vessel hove in sight.]

hove to the result of heaving to

How cheer ye? How are you?

Howell Davis a seaman who is captured by pirate

Ye Olde Seafaring Lexicon

Edward England and, because of his easy-going nature, gets along royally with the pirate crew whose captain, England, is uncharacteristically compassionate, imprisoned for three months by his own released crew for making friends with pirates, thereafter can't get work for his fouled reputation, and so becomes a pirate after all, but refuses to consort with dastardly captains such as Thomas Cocklyn

hull the bottom of the ship whereto is attached the keel

hull down far enough away so that the hull of the vessel is not visible over the horizon [only her masts may be seen]

huzzah! a shout of cheer or approval

Ye Olde Seafaring Lexicon

I

Ilanun, the dreaded pirates of Mindanao, Philippines

'in a clinch an' no knife to cut the seizin' hard up, desperate

in the offing likely to happen soon ['Storm's in the offing, messmate. Best batten down.']

inch of candle refers to establishing a time limit on something, auctioneers at Port Royal often use this technique when taking bids on prize vessels, once the auctioneer receives the highest bid for an item, he lights a candle and scores it one inch from the top, all wait for the candle to burn down to the mark, if no one offers a higher bid during the wait, the last bidder becomes the legal owner of the prize, by extension, You have little time [I gives ye a inch o' candle, sirrah! To yer dooty, dog!]

Indiaman a merchant of either East India Company [English or Dutch]

Indian corn maize

inst. the abbreviation for instant and meaning this month [We came into Port Royal the 2nd inst.]

instanter now, on the double [The captain will see ye instanter, sirrah!]

interloper a pirate, or, an enemy Navy ship carrying a Commission of Reprisal

Isthmus Treasure Ports the Spanish treasure ports on or near the Isthmus of Panama in the Caribbean to include Nombre de Dios, Porto Bello, Panama, and Cartagena

J

jack the flag showing a ship's nationality or persuasion, usually flown at the bow

Jack Rackam flag [Calico Jack] black field, white skull with crossed cutlasses aneath

Jack Tar affectionate appellation for any seaman

Jacob's ladder the rope ladder used to climb aboard ship

Jacques de Sores a French Huguenot pirate who attacks and burns Havana, Cuba in 1555, nicknamed 'The Exterminating Angel' ['L'Ange Exterminateur'], in 1570 he murders 40 Jesuit missionaries and tosses their bodies into the sea off Las Palmas in the Canary Islands, where crosses on the sea floor still mark the site at Malpique today

Jacqoutte Delahaye an African-French [Creole] buccaneer, active in the 1660's, hailed from Haiti and is described as a great beauty who becomes a pirate after her family is killed

Jamaica Discipline a code of laws adopted by buccaneers respecting the prize where the captain receives two shares, officers one and a half shares, and seamen one share in all captures, a forerunner of ship's articles

Jan Janszoon van Haarlem a pirate of the late 16th century who attacks Spanish ship while flying the Dutch flag and all others while flying the red half-moon of the Turks

jardin [French: garden] the head, a marine toilet usually no more than a hole cut in the decking at the head or bow of the ship which allows waste to go into the sea, the waves hopefully washing away what may not hit the water

jetsam goods cast overboard deliberately, as to

lighten a vessel or improve its stability in an emergency, sink where jettisoned or are washed ashore

jib triangular sail set on a stay extending from the head of the foremast to the bowsprit or the jibboom

jibboom spar forming an extension of the foremast and bowsprit

John Halsey a colonial American pirate who is active in the Atlantic and Indian Oceans during the early 17th century, although much of his life and career is unknown, he is recorded by Daniel Defoe in A General History of the Pyrates which states 'He was brave in his Person, courteous to all his Prisoners, lived beloved, and died regretted by his own People. His Grave was made in a garden of watermelons, and fenced in with Palisades to prevent his being rooted up by wild Hogs.'

John Julian was the first recorded Black pirate to operate in the New World, as the pilot of the pirate ship Whydah, a half-blood Mosquito Indian who joined Samuel Bellamy early in his brief, brilliant career, while on land, his skin made him nobody, on water, his skill made him important, eventually piloted the Whydah, which was the leading ship of Bellamy's fleet, was one of 30 to 50 people of African descent in the pirate crew, all treated as equals, Julian's life took a bad turn after he survived the Whydah wreck in 1717, jailed in Boston but was never indicted, but rather was sold into slavery and became 'Julian the Indian' bought by John Quincy, whose grandson, President John Quincy Adams, became a staunch abolitionist, a purported 'unruly slave,' he was sold to another owner and often tried to escape, during one escape attempt he killed a bounty hunter who was trying to catch him, executed in 1733

johns unknown people, or those considered

unimportant

John Ward [Warde] too known as Jack Ward, under his Muslim nom de guerre of Yusuf Reis [literally, 'Joe Admiral'] was a notorious English pirate ca. the turn of the 17th century who later became a Barbary corsair operating out of Tunis

jolly boat [French: jolle] a yawl

Jolly Roger [French: joli rouge, or 'pretty red'] the red Flag of No Quarter, later, the black flag with skull and crossed bones, or with various other death symbols designed to remind the pirates themselves of their impending deaths, and to frighten merchant or Navy vessels

jump ship to go absent without leave, desert, run

junk [Portuguese: junco from the Javanese djong, meaning ship] a flat-bottomed ship with no keel, a flat bow and a high stern, width is ca. a third of her length with a rudder that can be lowered or raised, providing fine steering capability, water-tight hull, two or three masts with square sails made from bamboo, rattan, or grass, capable of operating in any sea, originally designed by sea nymphs, too means old or inferior rope

jury mast a temporary mast replacing one lost overboard or broken [We found ourselves ashore searching for a trunk suitable for a jury mast.]

kaper any Dutch pirate

kedge anchors small anchors used to keep a ship from riding over her bow anchor in a change of tide or wind

keel the part of most vessels which allows the necessary slicing through the water, on most ships, the bow is too provided with a cutwater

keel-haul a punishment where a rope is tied to a sailor and then he [or she, as in the case of pirates] is hauled aneath the keel of the ship numerous times until the wrongdoer is either penitent or drowned, used too by the ancient Greeks

keep her in play to keep demanding that a fort or a ship strike colors or fight until one is done

ketch a two-masted vessel with square sails, from 100 to 250 tons burthen, bombards citadels, towns and other fortresses, square-rigged on the foremast and fore-and-aft rigged on the mainmast, which is stepped well aft [set back well aft of the ship]

key a small, sandy island

killing a man in cold blood dispatching a fellow pirate outside of a fight, and usually with no warning, according to ship's articles, normally punished by death

King's Commission a commission to a privateer to bring all pirates to justice

King William's War [1689-1697] the War of English Succession

kiss the gunner's daughter to acquiesce to the routine, and sometimes punishment, of being tied to a gun and flogged

Klaus Störtebeker leader of the Vitalian Brotherhood

Ye Olde Seafaring Lexicon

knave a ne'er-do-well, low-life, churl, bachlach [Irish], common appellation for any pirate

knight-errantry the Romantic way in which many soldiers and other landmen see piracy

knight-heads the two pieces of timber rising on either side of the bowsprit to secure its inner end

knocked onto beam-ends in a gale, to list either starboard or port to the extreme that the beams of the ship touch the water, too, to be bested in a fight [Twas then the blackguard hauled off an' knocked me on me beam-ends, he did!]

knock off to quit a piratical outfit whenever a company breaks the gang, one of the celebrated perks of life as a lawless sailor

knot one nautical mile per hour

know the ropes to understand or have a grasp of a job

kraken [Scandinavian] the feared giant squid, thought to be able to capsize the largest seagoing vessel

L

lade [1] to put cargo aboardship
lade [2] to bale water out of a ship
lading cargo
ladrones [Spanish: mercenaries, bandits] pirates
lagan anything sunk in the sea, but attached to a
buoy or the like so it can be recovered
lagoon [Latin] a deep, basin-like body of water with a
narrow entrance, often used by pirates for safety as
they careen their ships
Lancelot Blackburne pirate and Archbishop of
York
landfall land as seen from the water, or, the
expectation of land [Oh, God have mercy,
messmates! Landfall!]
land guns to move guns from a ship to land so as to
defend coastal territory [Land guns, lads. We're in
for warm work with the dogs this e'en!]
land ho! a cry of land sighted, often from the crow's
nest
landlocked when the land lies round about, so that
no point is open to the sea [We be landlock'd 'til low
tide, sure.]
landlubbers [land-lovers] landsmen
landsmen [landmen] those not having adopted a
seaman's life, inexperienced sailors, soldiers
land to when a ship lies at such a distance at sea that
she can only just discern land [We was just at land
to when we was come upon by the rakehells.]
langrel [langrace] pieces of iron, nails, bolts, etc.
placed in a thin casing and shot as anti-personnel
weapons, used almost always by privateers, as
pirates enjoy adding large numbers to their
complements, and the dead make poor looters

lantaka a type of swivel gun found on junks

larboard port, to the left side of the ship when facing the bow

lateen rig a triangular sail extended by a long spar slung to a low mast

latitude east/west

laudanum a solution of opium and alcohol used as a sedative or painkiller

launch a peculiar long-boat which is lower, longer and more flat-bottomed than the traditional style, less fit for sailing but better calculated for rowing and approaching a flat shore

lawful occasion lawful occupation

lay anchor drop anchor

lay her aboard to come alongside a ship in battle [Lay her aboard and ready for warm work, lads!]

lay the land to be without or lose sight of land [We're lay the land, Cap'n. I be takin' thieves watch this evening, sir.]

lay to [lie to] bring a ship into the wind and hold her stationary

league ca. 2.5 to 4.5 statute miles, or about 3 miles

learn the ropes [know the ropes] to gain the knowledge of the many miles of a ship's cordage making up her rigging

lee direction or side away from the wind, downwind

leech either vertical edge of a square sail, or, the after edge of a fore-and-aft sail

lee quarter the corner of the ship away from the wind

leeshore the shore upon which the leeward winds are blowing, a hazard for sailing craft, and especially in gale or hurricane winds

leeward ye side of the ship away from the winds

leeward winds blowing onto shore

leeway the room a ship needs to keep from being driven ashore

Ye Olde Seafaring Lexicon

Lesser Antilles the islands of the Caribbean to
   include the Virgin, Leeward, and Windward Islands,
   Trinidad, Barbados, Tobago, and all islands in the
   South Caribbean north of Venezuela
let go to free or cast off, too, to drop anchor
Letter of Marque a license allowing privateers to
   commandeer enemy vessels and to make war on
   other nations [He's missing the marque, Admiral!
   Nowhere on him, sir!]
let the cat out of the bag to say or do something to
   cause the cat-o'-nine-tails to be taken out of its
   leather or baize bag and perniciously employed
Libertaria a pirate colony formed by Madagascar
   pirates Thomas Tew and Captain Misson only three
   years after Tew had become a British privateer
lies land too when a ship can only discern land [The
   ship lies land too! We're doomed! Abandon ship!]
light of spy or spot [Yon tar in the crow's nest didst
   light of five piratical sloops yestreen! Ahoy, Billy
   Yarn! How be the weather?]
light pair o' heels a small, fast ship
lights lungs [Mind yer bearin', boy! He'll have yer
   lights an' liver!]
light upon to seize a ship in a piratical maneuver
Likedeelers successors of the disbanded Vitalian
   Brotherhood who share all booty equally, even with
   the poor people of the coasts which they ravage
like to have [been, done, etc.] meaning almost
   [Their rash decision like to have been their
   destruction or I like to have forgotten their date
   palms.]
limp in to come into port with damaged masts, sails,
   taking on water, etc.
Line, the Equator, customary for seamen to clean-
   shave whenever crossing it
linen neck cloths commonly worn by seamen to
   absorb sweat

Ye Olde Seafaring Lexicon

linen or cotton shirt worn at sea aneath the jacket or fearnought, usually white or off-white, though blue and white checks are common

lines the securing cables on a ship which are often cut by pirates upon boarding

list to involuntarily heel to port or starboard

list to starboard in port bad omen causing sailors to jump ship

lively there! the command to act quickly but carefully [Look lively!]

locker a chest for compact stowage of articles

lock, stock and barrel the entire gun, and so by extension, the whole thing

loggerhead the long-handled implement with an iron ball at one end which is heated and used to seal the pitch in deck seams, used as a weapon [see at loggerheads]

logwood wood of the logwood tree [haematoxylon campeachianum] producing a valuable red [purple] stain used for dying cloth, grown in Central America and lain low by logwood cutters, many of whom are former pirates

longboat carried aboard ship and used for traveling to and from ship, usually rowed, but sports a removable mast and sail, carries a complement of 25

long clothes landlubbin' clothes worn ashore, a suit of these often saves a merchant sailor from being pressed into the Navy when his ship comes into port

longitude north/south

Long Tom a heavy swivel gun

longship the square-rigged ship of Scandinavia

lookout the sailor in charge of watching for land, ships, or upsetting weather

loose cannon a cannon aboardship which has broken loose of its moorings, physically dangerous in a storm, thus, anybody who defies authority to the detriment of the crew

looter pirate

lorcha [Chinese] a light Chinese vessel with a European-style hull, but used as a junk

los corsarios luteranos [Spanish] Protestant ['Lutheran'] pirates, meaning rovers who attack coastal villages with no intent other than to rape and pillage, suggesting that Catholic pirates are somehow more orderly and gentlemanly in their actions, if not altogether more righteous or 'in the right'— and indeed, Spanish seamen are appalled at the roguish capitalistic practice of 'buying cheap and selling dear' [fencing], which on the far end of the 'buying' scale incorporates outright theft of the product to be resold

lost wrecked [shipwrecked]

lower sail to take down sail

lubberly of landlubbers [land-lovers], not of the sea or maritime ideas

lucky shark fin, the often attached at the very tip of the jibboom

luff to turn a ship closer to the wind, to keep a ship's head windward [luffed to]

lugger a light-heeled ship

lull the downbeat of a ship as she shakes the wind out of a sail

lurking places pirate hideouts

lying ahull ship at hull

lying to [try, or lie-a-try] in a severe storm, to remain in the trough or hollow of the waves by reducing sail, and in rarer cases lying under bare boles, too, the position a ship finds herself in after being brought to

M

macaroni [Italian] the style of the fop or dandy often characterized by extremely stylish dress to include macaroni stockings, a waistcoat, a brightly-colored silk sash for the waist, a pocket-watch and fob, lace for the throat and a feather in the hat, among other accessories, a style greatly loved by pirates, especially while boarding

macaroni stockings black and white vertical striped stockings worn with knickerbockers by fops and dandies, or worn with sailors' petticoats by pirates

Madagascar a renowned pirate haven

Madeiraman merchant trading with the Madeira Islands of the northwest coast of Africa

magazine the storage area for gunpowder and ammunition

Magister Wigbold also called 'Master of the Seven Arts,' is a German pirate who belongs to the famous Likedeeler gang

mainmast the middle mast of a three-masted ship, or the second mast of a two-master

main-royal the sail on the mainmast above the topgallant, or the fourth sail in ascending order from the deck

mainsheet the rope at the lower corner of the mainsail for regulating its position

maintain point to not be blown off course

maintop crow's nest

main-topsail a sail on the mainmast above the mainsail, or the second sail in ascending order from the deck on the ship's primary mast

mainyard the yard of a mainsail

make a market out of her to take all that is worth

anything out of a ship

make free with to have wanton sexual relations with, often permissible

make sail open the sails

make up market to find other prizes to fill out the present needs

mal de mer seasickness

Malta from 1530-1798 considered a dangerous haven of 'corsairs parading crosses'

man any ship with the name of her port of origin as a common noun prefix, thus, Virginiaman, Carolinaman, Bristolman, Madeiraman, Indiaman, etc.

Manannán meic Lir [Irish] the Irish name for Poseidon

manchuas [Bharatan] a single-masted cargo boat used on the Malabar coast of India

man the yard arms! the command to prepare for action concerning sail change at the yards

man-o-war a first- through fourth-rate ship, ship-of-the-line, over 100 guns, ca. 1,000 tons and three square-rigged masts except for a lateen rig on her aft-mast

manumission [French] freedom from slavery [The coffin Colleen's Pride, belonging to slaver Captain Wm. Saintly, was manumissioned by Spanish privateers on the 28th inst.]

Maria Lindsey an English pirate with her husband Eric Cobham who made her base in Newfoundland, known for giving 'no quarter,' all captured crews are killed and the ships sunk, famous for her cruelty, including using survivors for target practice

mariner any seaman

maritime literally, 'ocean time', of the ocean or about it

market two or more ships coming together to buy, sell or trade goods

marlinspike a steel rod, tapered to a point at one
end, the other usually with a wider head, used to
open up the strands of a rope in order to tuck
another strand under, also used in splicing rope

marlinspike seamanship a general term referring
to the working of rope, cable, etc., encompasses
tying of knots, bends, lashing, and other activities,
sailors often take great pride in these skills

maroon to put a sailor on a desert island with a
pistol, a few shot, some powder, and a skin or two of
water

marooners pirates

Marshalsea Prison, London where pirates
marshaled at sea are usually confined

mast the part of the ship carrying the sail with the
assistance of yards and cordage

Master the commander or captain of a ship, or, in
many cases, the navigator

Master-at-Arms the Naval ship's police officer
whose job on pirate ships is handled by the
Quartermaster

Master Gunner the seaman responsible for all guns
and ammunition including sifting the powder to
keep it dry and keeping its elements of saltpeter
[potassium nitrate], charcoal, and sulphur from
separating, too, responsible for keeping all metal
shot free from rust

match a slow-burning wick or cord used to light
cannon, pots of powder, etc.

Mather, Cotton an Ordinary Confessor for
condemned British pirates, witch-hunter, and
founder of Yale University

mechanic [factor] any artisan such as a cooper,
mason, millwright, cartwright, thatcher, armorer
[blacksmith], carpenter, etc.

menchew a single-masted vessel, usually a cargo
boat, much used on the coast of Malabar

Ye Olde Seafaring Lexicon

'men of honor' pirates
merchant [merchantman] a pink
meridian [Latin] any point on the globe
merry fellow an ignorant [ignoramus] or
  uneducated man often found in the company of
  pirates, and sometimes making up the majority of
  the crew
merry yarn a good story
mess any meal
messmate a term of endearment among sailors
Mestizo [Spanish] a person of both Spanish and
  American Indian blood, common among pirates
mettle the ability of a battery of guns
midline [centerline] an imaginary line drawn from
  bow to stern which equally divides the ship in two
  parts
mid-ocean at sea
midshipman a student in a Naval academy
midships amidships
minister a word unlucky to be said at sea, as well as
  church, chapel, and manse, too clergymen
  themselves are bad luck at sea [see cold iron]
Miss Taylor white wine
mizzenmast the mast closest to the stern
Modyford, Thomas the crooked governor of
  Jamaica during the height of Henry Morgan's
  buccaneering activities
moidore [Portuguese] Portuguese gold coin current
  in the 17th century, from moeda d'ouro meaning
  money of gold
monkey a small cannon
monkey jacket a short waist jacket worn by
  midshipmen
mooring securing a ship at port
Morgan, Captain Henry a highly honored
  Jamaican buccaneer who, because [unlike most
  pirates] he saved his money and went on to become

a successful capitalist, a contemporary of the relatively unknown St. Augustine, Florida raider Robert Searle

mortification when living tissue becomes necrotic or gangrenous, a common malady aboardship

Mother Carey's chickens sea petrels, any of various long-winged birds flying far from land believed to portend stormy weather if flying close to a ship, thus, storm petrels

mounted guns cannon mounted on wooden, wheeled carriages

much execution amongst men great carnage during battle

Muircartach a hag of the sea who is bald with a coal-colored face and one goggly eye placed in the middle of her forehead

mum this popular ale is made from wheat and oat malts and flavored with herbs, originates in Germany where it is called mumme, the Dutch refer to it as mom

murderer a 15th century swivel cannon

music common on pirate ships for entertainment, compulsorily played during action to demoralize the enemy and to get the swashbucklers jigging to a good tune as they deftly cut out hearts and aim cannons at the heads of bound prisoners, shooting their brains out at the closest possible range

musket common seaman's weapon

muster all hands for roll call

mutineers sailors who mutiny against a captain and his supporting officers, often having no remaining option but piracy

myrmidon [Greek: mermidon] an unquestioning follower or subordinate who blindly carries out orders, often found aboard ships piratical or otherwise

N

nabob [Hindi] a successful pirate-lord living
fabulously off of booty

nail up to spike a cannon so it can't be shot

nao Portuguese and Spanish word for the carrack

nautical mile 6,080 feet

navigator [sailing master] in charge of navigation,
directs the course and maintains waggoners, maps,
and instruments necessary for navigation, often
forced into pirate service upon fear of death

neap tides those tides which fall when the Moon is in
her second and last quarter, and are neither so high
nor low, as Spring Tides [The ship is beneaped,
Cap'n Shagg. We'll sail to Neverland this night,
sure.]

Neverland sailors' misnomic euphemism for
netherlands, or unknown outlands, and by
extension, nowhere

Newgate Prison a jail [British: gaol] holding mostly
thieves and murderers, but housing the occasional
pirate [to the latter's chagrin, as he carries an
extremely low opinion of the housebreak and
pickpocket], the prison to which pirates who will not
plead are taken and pressed in the press yard,
ostensibly so that they will plead, but the end result
is fatal more often than not

New Providence an island in the Bahamas which
becomes the new pirate haven after 1714

Nicholas Brown an English pirate active off the
coast of Jamaica during the early 18th century,
although accepting a royal pardon, he continues
raiding ships until his capture by childhood friend
Captain John Drudge, eventually dies of wounds
received during his capture, Drudge decapitates him

and pickles his head

Ninth Wave a mythic longitude in the Western Sea where lies Avalon

nocturnal midnight determined by using this navigation tool which tells the time of night by the rotation of stars around the celestial pole

nom de guerre [French] literally, a 'battle name,' such as Black Bart or Calico Jack or Blackbeard

no prey, no pay [no purchase, no pay] the unwritten article for every piratical endeavor

no quarter no mercy, symbolized by a red flag

no room to swing a cat the entire ship's company is required to witness floggings, and often crowds in close to get a good view of the proceedings, when the boatswain's mate readies to employ the cat, there may not be enough room for him to get a good swing in

Nortada [Portuguese] the North Wind

North Star looked for in the Northern Hemisphere as a navigational tool

no skin off my back [no sweat off my back] I've done nothing to deserve the lash or I'm above getting the cat or, more figuratively and by extension, It makes no difference to me

O

oakum hemp fiber from old rope impregnated with tar, used to caulk or waterproof a ship

oarports ports in galleys [and some other ships] for the sweeps

Ocracoke Island [Ocacock on older maps] an island off the coast of North Carolina between Pamlico Sound and the Atlantic where Blackbeard makes his port, possibly the island of Croatan where the Roanoke Island colony is by some thought to have moved

offing distant part of the sea beyond the anchoring ground but still visible from the shore, view of open sea from land, early texts too refer to it as 'offen' or 'offin', a person watching out for a ship first sees it approaching when it is 'in the offing' and expected to dock soon, by extension, something that is 'in the offing' isn't happening now or even in a minute or two, but will inevitably happen before long

off soundings any place where the water is too deep for the depth to be measured with a weighted line

offward from the shore

Oggin the sea

Oglethorpe, James British philanthropist and sea captain responsible for the brutal attack on the freed slave town of Gracia Real de Santa Teresa de Mose situated just north of St. Augustine, Florida

Olivier Levasseur a pirate nicknamed La Buse or La Bouche [The Buzzard] in his early days, called thus because of the speed with which he threw himself on his enemies, most famous for a cryptogram detailing a buried treasure yet undiscovered

on account living the life of a pirate

on float to come off ground [Aye, sir! We've run

aground, sir, an' it'll be night now afore we're on
float!]

open fire to engage fully with gunfire

ordinary a restaurant or eating-house

Ordinary Confessor a priest or pastor assigned to
hear the private confessions of condemned pirates,
and then, as in the case of Cotton Mather,
publicizing these confessions after the unfortunates'
dispatching

ordinary seaman a sailor with limited experience

ordnance a ship's weapons, used parsimoniously by
pirates so as not to damage a prize

original [French] origin [I do not know the original
o' the rover, sir, but methinks he mayest be
Jamaican.]

orlop the lowest deck above the bilges of a ship, at
water level or below the waterline, where powder
and shot ride

out at elbows poor, having little or nothing

out of the way hiding, usually from prosecution

outward bound seaward

overbear the act of sailing downwind directly at
another ship, usually an enemy, thus diverting the
wind from her sails, viz., to be overbearing

overset to lose a ship while she is careened by having
her topple over and snap her masts, etc.

overwhelm [over helm] to capsize or sink as a result
of heavy sea [As the storm raged in, we were soon
overwhelmed.]

Ye Olde Seafaring Lexicon

P

painter a rope at the bow of a boat

pannikin a metal cup

pantaloons tight trousers fastened below the calf

panyarr the act of Africans stealing Europeans [who have come as slavers] and making them slaves in Africa

parcel passel, gang of pirates

parley [French] to discuss terms with an enemy, can be called by captives in hopes of buying time or coming to terms

part the bear skin two pirate leaders, of equal popularity with the crew, dividing up their authority equally and creating two separate pirate companies

patareroes [Spanish] muzzle-loading mortars which fire scatter-shot, stones, spikes, nails, glass and other debris

patois [French] lingo, lingua franca

pay caulk

pay out to let anchor cable out

Peace of Utrecht [Treaty of Utrecht] signed April 1713, bringing an end to the War of Spanish Succession [Queen Anne's War]

peacoat [pea jacket] a heavy woolen double-breasted jacket worn by sailors [coined 1721]

Pedro Menéndez de Avilés [Menéndez] a 16th century Spanish pirate most notable for his founding of St. Augustine, Florida in 1565 [52 years after the land's conquering by Juan Ponce de Leon] and the destruction of the French settlement of Fort Caroline [today known as Jacksonville]

Peg Leg a French pirate of the mid-16th century

pennant a long, narrow and normally triangular flag mostly used for signaling or decoration

per diem [Latin] literally, each day [We've one bottle o' water per diem, Cap'n, an'll perish directly without more!]

perjured persons privateers under oath who have turned pirate

Peter Easton a pirate of the early 17th century who operates along the Newfoundland coastline between Harbour Grace and Ferryland, one of the most successful of all pirates, he controls such seapower that no sovereign or state can afford to ignore him, and he is never overtaken by any commissioned to hunt him

Philistines 3:8 a 'Biblical scripture' quoted by the sanctimonious Judge Trot to pirate captain Major Stede Bonnet, found in Captain Charles Johnson's A General History Of The Robberies & Murders Of The Most Notorious Pyrates.

picarón [Spanish] pirate, picaroon, pickaroon, from the Spanish word for rascal, too applied to a form of verse about pirates which is satirical or humorous

pickle to rub salt or salted vinegar into lashes, which exacerbates the pain but helps to heal the wounds by killing bacteria

pick up catch a wind

piece small arms, pistol [flintlock]

pieces-of-eight [eight reales or pesos] silver mined by Incan slaves from the mountain of Potosi, in Peru and made into a 'piece-of-eight' real, often cut into two, four, or eight pieces, thus pieces of eight

pierced hull a hull designed for gunports

Pier Gerlofs Donia of Kimswerd a 16th century Frisian warrior, pirate, freedom fighter and folk hero remembered for his impressive physique

pilfer to rifle through and take lading, etc., at will

pillage to raid and sack a target on shore

piloting sailing within sight of land

pilot of the watch the seaman in charge of compass

and course

Pilot of the World, the spirit believed by sailors to
come to their aid in dire circumstances, usually
accompanied by a crew of angelic beings who can
sail

pink two classes: [1] small, flat-bottomed ship with a
narrow stern whose name is derived from the Italian
pinco and used in the Mediterranean as a cargo ship,
[2] in the Atlantic, any small, square-rigged ship
with a narrow stern used as a merchantman and
warship whose name is derived from the Dutch
word pincke

pinnace a boat rowed with eight oars and usually
thinner, longer, and shallower than a yawl, generally
used as a tender, can too be a larger, two-masted
craft, any of various ship's boats

pipe a large cask of varying capacity, but more
precisely of 126 gallons, used to hold wine and oil

pipe down on Navy ships, lights out and silence are
the last call of the boatswain's pipe at the end of the
day, i.e., the unspoken command to be quiet

pipe up! speak up

piracy specifically, taking things which do not belong
to the taker, generally, and so more importantly, the
anarchic spirit of freedom against any paradigm
built upon false ideologies which oppress the people

piragua [Spanish: pirogue, perigua, periaga,
periangar, pettiauga, pettiaga] a masted, flat-
bottomed boat dugout from a tree trunk, or made of
two halves of a large tree, often used stealthily by
pirates to maneuver into villages settled along
creeks and rivers, and into hidden coves and
lagoons, can carry ca. thirty barrels

pirate [pyrate] an English word derived from the
Middle Latin piratia, which itself comes from the
Latin Greek peirateia, which hails from the Greek
[peirates] from the root [peiran] meaning to attempt

Ye Olde Seafaring Lexicon

pirate articles [ship's articles] a set of rules and provisions drawn up by the captain and quartermaster and strictly enforced aboardship, sworn to with a hand on a Bible or, if the Good Book isn't available, a hatchet [which is sometimes preferred as a sacrilegious act]

Pirate March of 1683, the a little-known pirate attack on St. Augustine, Florida

pirate society a classic textbook Leveling society [Levelers] where all men are regarded as equal

piratical account the life of piracy

piratical discharge in writing 10 lashes on the back from every man aboardship

pistol proof the bullying mechanism of fear used by certain pirate captains, such as Blackbeard and Bartholomew Roberts [Black Bart] in order to make his position more than a mere figurehead to be trampled upon by an unruly crew

pistol [Spanish: pistole] any of the several gold coins of Europe of approximately the same value as the Spanish version

pitch when the stern and head [bow] plunge alternately into the sea during storms instead of rolling, thus, the old salt's crusty remark 'Roll, roll ye son of a bitch! The more ye roll, the less ye'll pitch!'

pitched deck a deck covered with pitch or tar for better traction, but highly flammable, therefore, making a sanded deck is the better choice, or one of cork if available

plain sailing undisturbed sailing, easy

Plate Fleet the Spanish Treasure Fleet

play before [the ship] the act of a pressed musician, sometimes a bagpiper, as the pirate ship chases or apprehends a prize

play the whole game cheat all you can

plough the great salt field ne'er sown the act of

sailing the high seas

plum duff pudding made with flour, lard, sugar, and raisins or currants

plunder [n.] booty, [v.] to go after booty

ply to windward to seek security with the winds away from enemy vessels

plying turning to windward

point to position the head of a vessel in a specific direction relative to the wind

pointing handsome headed into good waters [We're pointin' handsome now, sir!]

pompions [English] pumpkins

Ponce de León conquistador conquering Florida in 1513 at the site to later become known as St. Augustine

pooped to be swamped at the poop deck by a heavy following sea

poop deck the stern, or, an enclosed superstructure at the stern above the quarterdeck or main deck

post duty, or the position of duty

port [larboard] the left side of an oceangoing craft facing forward, the side of a ship turned to the quay in port because, on Viking ships, the steerboard [starboard] is on the right and so lies vulnerable, to put to the left, too, a seaport

port-o-call a favorite port, or, a port of necessity

Port Royal the center of shipping commerce in Jamaica until an earthquake on June 7, 1692 largely destroyed it, causing two thirds of the city to sink into the Caribbean Sea

pots of powder incendiary devices made of clay pots filled with gunpowder which are lit and thrown

pound the British unit of monetary measurement

powder [black powder] a mixture of saltpeter [potassium nitrate], charcoal, and sulphur

powder house a family dwelling or business covertly housing the official store of powder and shot to defend the city

powder monkey a gunner's assistant, usually a young boy

poxed diseased, often used as an insult

prahu [Indonesian] the shallow-draft canoe of the Ilanun Indonesian pirates, rowed by slaves

prayer book small block of sandstone used to scrub the hard-to-reach portions of the deck [while on the knees, thus the name: compare to Bible]

preferment the act of turning pirate because life as a beggar, an ordinary seaman, or a private in the Navy does not suite the present needs, or, an officer position on a ship [He was voted into gunner preferment for his former experience on the Ditchwitch.]

present death [1] suicide, often chosen over starvation, dying of thirst, or official embarrassment because of capture by pirates

present death [2] immediate death for resistance, or no quarter

presidio [Spanish] a Spanish fortress

press to force a man into maritime duty, whether this act be 'lawful' or otherwise

press gang officials of the Navy under the leadership of a lieutenant who prowl highways, byways, towns, downs [farms], and cities of England pressing, or forcing, seamen into duty, landsmen [landlubbers] with no sea experience are not often pressed, and for good reason

press of sail an unintentional heel port or starboard, a list in high wind

press yard the yard at Newgate Prison where pirates who refuse to plead are pressed to death by having weights [stones, etc.] piled on their prostrate bodies until death occurs by suffocation, which may take days, many pirates upon hearing of this torture change their minds and either plead guilty or not guilty, nolo contendere not instituted until 1872 ['no contention', meaning that the criminal, while not admitting guilt, is subject to conviction but may deny the charges in a second proceeding]

pretty cows llamas

preventor-shrouds extra shrouds to take strain off the mast during stormy conditions

private adventure merchandise on a ship privately owned by a captain or other crew-member, as opposed to merchandise owned by the ship's owner or an enterprising merchant entrepreneur

private stock on Navy vessels, the better class of wine or other strong drink reserved for the Admiral, Captain, and other officers

privateer a seaman given Letters of Marque, a Commission of Reprisal and/or a King's Commission by his government, a legalized pirate, infamous practitioners include Captain Kidd and Francis Drake, flies the Black Jack when attacking other nations, a ship carrying such piratical opportunists

prize a stolen vessel

prize crew, the crew of pirates ferried over by the victims that the latter may study the ship's manifest and secure cargo

provided for sentenced to hang for piracy

provisioned outfitted for a voyage

prow the nose of a ship

Psellusian Phantoms spectres of whom little is known, other than they haunt ships lost at sea

pull to row

punch house what the English called a brothel, originally referred to any low-class drinking establishment, one traveler to Port Royal is reported to have believed punch houses consisted of 'such a crew of vile strumpets and common prostitutes that 'tis almost impossible to civilize [the town]'

purchase the overtaking and/or commandeering of a merchant or other ship, or, the pillage of a coastal village or trading port

push the boat out to spend more than a body is normally accustomed to doing, often to mark a special occasion

push up to sail north

put about the command to turn round, change course or direction, go on another tack

put affairs in a proper disposition aboard to commandeer a craft and subdue her captain and crew

put in drop anchor

put to sea to embark on a voyage

quarter mercy, to refrain from killing somebody, often with the design to coerce them into piracy, use them as ransom or sell them as slaves, among other pirates of high moral standing, captain Howell Davis threatens death to his own men if they refuse to show quarter to those calling for it

quarterdeck a deck stretching from the stern amidships, the place from which the ship's officers control the vessel

quartermaster in piracy, nearly equal to the captain, has the authority to order the captain in all matters outside of chase and actual battle, elected by the crew to represent their interests and receives an extra share of the booty when it is divided, maintains order aboard ship, settles quarrels, and distributes food and other essentials, and measures off the 20 paces for any pistol duel between two crewmen, receives his title from his main duty, which is to either give or withhold quarter

quay [pronounced key] a port dock, quayside

Queen Ann's Revenge Blackbeard's flagship

Queen Anne's War or the War of Spanish Succession [1701-1713]

queue a sailor's pigtail, usually tarred

quintal a weight equal to 100 pounds

R

race-built galleon a small, sleek British derivative of the Spanish galleon avoiding cumbersome, towering superstructures, an example is Drake's Golden Hind

rail the planed timber planking superior to the gunwale and to which are attached swivel guns [such as murderers]

rais a sea captain in the service of the Barbary corsairs

raise to come to [We raised the Cape at last!]

raking to fire at a vessel's stern, the weakest part of the ship

ramming not an attractive option for piratical mercenaries intent upon commandeering a booty-filled victim vessel

rammer the cannon ramrod

ramrod rammer

rapine a plundering act of piracy

rate warships are grouped into 6 categories according to their number of guns, first-rate, 100, second-rate, 90, third-rate, 70-80, fourth-rate, 50-65, fifth-rate, 25-40, sixth-rate, 10-25, first- through fourth-rates are known as ships-of-the-line or man-o-wars because they can take their places in lines of battle

rations daily food and drink

ratlines small lines of rope fastened across a ship's shrouds and used as a ladder to climb into the rigging

rattan the rough leaves of a sturdy Malaysian palm used for wickerwork and the 'three sisters'

Rawhead and Bloodybones a gruesome monster living in the pools of Ireland [and later in the swamps and backwoods of the North American

Ye Olde Seafaring Lexicon

Deep South], since the 16th century, supposedly an
inspiration for the Jolly Roger

reach the distance between the two nearest points of
land, on the same shore [What be the reach, sir, and
in your surmise can we make it without detection?]

Read, Mary sailed and pirated with Calico Jack,
pardoned because she is found to be heavy with
child

ready about the command to tack

real [Spanish] a Spanish silver coin pronounced reé-
al or reé-al-ay, and is sometimes spelled reale, rial,
riyal and ryal. A piece-of-eight is the equivalent of
eight reals.

recoil the dangerous reaction of a fired cannon

red deck a deck painted such so that the sailors won't
see the blood during battle

reef a part of a sail taken in or let out in regulating
size, reduction in sail area by rolling or folding a
portion, to lower or bring inboard a spar wholly or
partially, the end result is called a reefer

refit to repair a ship

reins the kidneys or lower part of the back, often a
point of attack in battle

rencontre [French] a hostile encounter or battle

repair on board the command to return to ship

report the deafening sound of a cannon being fired

Reprisal the System of Rights issued by monarchs to
owners of ships enduring loss whereby said owners
may sail against other nations, Letters of Marque
follow this system [Commission of Reprisal]

residue the remaining crew of a company of pirates
whose majority have opted to knock off

restricted waters naturally difficult waters to
maneuver through such as creeks, rivers, etc.

retire turn in

return a compliment to return fire

ribs the internal structure of the hull

Ye Olde Seafaring Lexicon

Richard Worley flag the classic Jolly Roger with crossed bones behind a smiling skull

rickets a disease characterized by soft and deformed bones because of not being able to assimilate calcium and phosphorous for the lack of vitamin D or sunlight [therefore not a problem once sailors arrive in the Caribbean or other tropical latitudes]

ride betwixt wind and tide when the wind and tide are contrary, and have equal power

rifle to plunder

rigger's loft compartment where extra rigging is kept

rigging rope, block-and-tackle, etc.

right directly in just a minute or not very long from now [We'll be comin' ta port right d'rectly]

road [roadstead] a protected area near shore and not enclosed as a harbor where ships may anchor

Roaring Forties, the West Winds below the Cape

Robert Searle [aka Robert Searles] a classic Jamaican English buccaneer [after England drove the Spanish from the island] who in May 1668 leads a massacre in St. Augustine, Florida against the Spanish settlers there, this act completely eclipsed by fellow Jamaican buccaneer Henry Morgan's sacking of the highly-fortified Spanish city of Porto Bello, Panama on July 11th and 12th of this same year

Robin Hood's Bay a Medieval village on the coast of Yorkshire that, during the Napoleonic Wars, collectively took to smuggling, any resident of this village who will not smuggle is asked to leave, though their people have been residents as long or longer than the pirating clans living there

Roche Braziliano drunken and debauched, he threatens to shoot anyone who will not drink with him, roasted alive two Spanish farmers on wooden spits after they refused to hand over their pigs,

treats his Spanish prisoners barbarously, typically
cutting off their limbs or roasting them alive over a
spit

rod a measurement equal to 16.5 feet or 5.5 yards

Rogers, Woodes an ex-pirate pirate-hunter
neglected and unrewarded by Britain for his royal
efforts

rolling when a ship rocks or sways from side to side
during a storm [see pitch]

Rolling Deep, the high seas

roll masts out to accidentally and disastrously heel
over in a storm

room place [n.] [Cap'n Blackweather made John
Hang bosun in Timmy Smith's room!]

rope's end flogging [Ye'll meet rope's end for that,
laddie.]

roundabouts [cackle fruit] eggs [this word being
unlucky aboard ship]

round house a cabin in the aft of the quarterdeck
having the poop as its roof

round robin a written petition of grievance
whereupon the names of the sailors have been
penned in a circle so as to cover the originator or
ring-leaders of the complaint, thus, a flummoxing
situation

round shot a cannon ball

rove to pass ropes or cable through a hole, such as a
hawsehole

rover [Anglo-Dutch] robber, pirate

royal the sail above the topgallant, or the fourth sail
in ascending order from the deck

Royal African Company the British government-
sanctioned slave trade company holding the
monopoly, by the end of the 17th century had
constructed 8 forts along the West African coast

rua chalom Siamese [Thai] junk

rudder ship's implement attached to the keel at stern

and acting much like a fish's tail

rullock the cutaway or notch on the side rail of the boat from which oars would pivot

rum [1] imbibed by pirates more often than the heavily rationed [and dangerous] water

rum [2] an odd or strange man [Aye, he's a rum fella, he.]

run to leave ship without permission, desert ship, jump ship

runagate renegade, pirate, rakehell, caballer, turncoat, traitor, perjured person, pirate

run at low game to make fewer attempts at capture for lack of a full pirate crew [Aye, we'll run at low game, messmates, 'til we build complement.]

running free when the wind blows from astern

running gear the working parts of the rigging

running the gauntlet the punishment of running through two lines of Navy seamen and being drubbed, or hit with sticks or stout pieces of rope, abolished in 1806

running the hazard of the neck risking hanging by continuing in piracy

running their easting down a ship catching the Roaring Forties to India

ruse de guerre [French] flying whatever flag necessary for survival or plunder, any diversion, trickery, or ploy employed during wartime, or by pirates anytime

S

sad dog scoundrel, pirate

sack to pillage or plunder

Sack of Cartagena, the [May 1689] the last major buccaneering endeavor before the advent of the Golden Age of Piracy

sail ho! exclamation when a ship is spotted

sailors' petticoats flaring canvas pants reaching just below the knee commonly worn as standard dress for seamen

saker basic shipboard armament of the 17th century, shoots 9-pounders as many as 4,000 yards [2.3 miles], utilized in broadsides and single fire to propel chain and hot shot aimed at sails to set them aflame

salamander a slow-burning wick or cord used to light cannons

salmagundi [French: salmagonde, salmagondis, solomongundy, salmagonde] a pirate specialty of meat, pickled herring, boiled eggs, vegetables, wine, oil, vinegar, salt, and pepper

salt [old salt] an experienced seaman, salty dog

Samuel Bellamy aka 'Black Sam' Bellamy, is a formidable pirate in the early 18th century, though his career as a pirate captain lasts less than one year, Bellamy and his crew capture more than 50 ships before his death at the age of 29, called 'Black Sam' because he eschews the fashionable powdered wig in favor of tying his long black hair back with a simple band, becomes known for his mercy and generosity toward those he captures on his raids, this reputation gains him the second nickname of the 'Prince of Pirates,' and his crew call themselves 'Robin Hood's Band.'

sanded deck a deck sanded for better traction and preferable to pitched or corked decks, both of which provide the hazards of fire and stumbling, respectively

sand glass [hourglass or ampoletta] time aboard ship was measured by this instrument, the ship's boy turns the glass every half-hour in order to measure time until his watch ends, because this instrument is not an accurate measurement of time, it is checked at regular intervals against sunrise, sunset, or midnight

sans pitié [French: without pity] a pirate flag with a black field adorned with a skull and crossbones to the left and to the right a man with a cutlass and an hourglass

schooner narrow hull, two masts and less than 100 tons, rigged with two large sails suspended from spars reaching from the top of the mast toward the stern, other sails sometimes added, including a large headsail attached to the bowsprit, shallow-draft allowing her to navigate and remain in shallow coves awaiting prey, very fast and large enough to carry a plentiful crew

scouse [Scandinavian: lobscouse] salt meat, potatoes, onions, broken hardtack and spices boiled as a stew

scrimshaw carvings on whale ivory or walrus tusks, routinely done by sailors, and especially by whalers, while at sea

scriven [scrivener] the clerk on a merchant ship

scrutoire [Spanish: escritoire] a writing desk, often found in the captain's quarters

scud [1] [n.] ocean spray carried swiftly by the wind

scud [2] [v.] to sail along quickly

scupper [1] an opening cut through the waterway and bulwarks of a ship to allow water and other fluids on the deck to flow overboard, and so by extension the angry expression 'Scupper that!'

scupper [2] to intentionally sink a ship

scurvy a disease marked by spongy gums, loose teeth, bleeding into the skin and mucous membranes, aching joints and body sores caused by a lack of vitamin C [therefore hardly a problem in the ascorbic acid-rich Caribbean and other tropical climes]

scuttle [1] to sink a ship intentionally

scuttle [2] a covered hatchway or opening in the deck large enough for a man to pass through

scuttlebutt a cask on shipboard ostensibly containing fresh water, thus, by extension, the latest news shared over this water barrel

sea banditti pirates

Sea Beggars Dutch pirates of the Dutch East India Company

sea bread hardtack, sea biscuits

sea breeze a cooling breeze blowing usually in the daytime inland from the sea

sea chanteys [shanteys or chanteys] easy-to-learn songs the chanteyman [shanteyman] sings to keep the working sailors both lively and entertained

sea coat a long, blue woolen coat worn by Navy admirals

sea cow manatee

sea dog the marine creature which in the 1560's became commonly known as the 'shark,' too, an Elizabethan seaman, such as the pyrate Francis Drake, sea rover

Sea Dyaks headhunting Indonesian pirates who use a variant of the prahu called the bangkong, most feared of the East Indian pirates

seafarer a mariner

seagirt surrounded by the sea [Aye, we be seagirt now, boyo! Before the mast with ye then!]

sea hog a porpoise

sea horses walruses, eaten as food

Ye Olde Seafaring Lexicon

sea king a Norse pirate king

sea legs the ability to walk steadily aboardship and without the added discomfort of seasickness [The lad's got his sea legs now. He'll be a salty dog soon enough.]

Sea of Darkness the tropical waters off the west coast of Africa where, when ventured, white men turn black

Sea of Sore Heads an' Sore Hearts the dangerous English Channel

Sea Rovers Elizabethan pirates, Sea Dogs

Robert Searles, Robert aka Robert Searles, Jamaican pirate who led a massacre at St. Augustine, Florida on May 29, 1668, after which the massive coquina Castillo de San Marcos was built (by Indian slave labor) to protect the town from other raids

sea store provisions for a lengthy venture at sea

sea virgin a mermaid, siren

sea witches the ghosts of dead witches who lurk up and down coasts cursing ships and bringing up storms, Francis Drake is said to have sold his soul to the Devil in order to be able to invoke these dastardly hags

sea wolves seals

Second Dutch War [1664-1667] when English buccaneers, acting as privateers, continuously attack the Dutch-claimed islands of Saba and St. Eustatius

seel when on a sudden a ship lies down and tumbles from side to side [Criost! She seels now, cap'n!]

see ye to Davy Jones to threaten to kill somebody [Ye'd best batten yer hatch, lad. Black Sam will see ye to Davy Jones in a twinkle o' yer deadlights.]

seized to ye shrouds a punishment or torture involving tying the sailor or victim to the shrouds

Selkirk, Alexander a mariner marooned on Juan Fernandez Island in the Pacific for four years, Daniel

Ye Olde Seafaring Lexicon

Defoe's 'Robinson Crusoe' character is based on him, discovered in February 1709 by buccaneer Woodes Rogers, who later becomes a pirate-hunter and governor of the Bahamas

send when a ship's head or stern falls deep in the Hollow of the Sea, commonly called the Trough of the Sea, and by extension, bewilderment [Aye, the lass sends me, Jack Trumpet, an' I canna keep her outta me noggin.]

sepsis [Latin] a major cause of death among seamen, when even a minor scrape or cut goes septic

set the distance a current has taken a ship

set sail to begin a sailing venture

1714 the end of the War of Spanish Succession creating peace between the controlling nations and many of out-of-work Navy seamen, who turn to piracy over going home to poverty or to begin their lives all over again

sextant an instrument for measuring angular distances to observe altitudes of celestial bodies so as to ascertain latitudes and longitudes

shake a leg when in port, the crew and their women sleep in hammocks, slung on hooks, when the bosun rouses out the crew for a sail change or other work he yells 'Shake a leg!', he can then tell by the leg if the sleeper is a crewman who needs rolling out

shape a course to plan a course of travel

shallop [French] a large boat with one or two masts, propelled by oars or sails and rigged like a schooner

shallow-draft a small vessel able to skirt shoals and sandbars and navigate into channels, inlets, creeks, rivers, and shallow coves

shebec [Arabic: xebec] a vessel favored among Barbary pirates, fast, stable and large, can reach 200 tons and carry from 4 to 24 cannon and 60 to 200 crewmen, a pronounced overhanging bow and stern, and three lateen-rigged masts, both sailed and rowed

sheet a rope made fast to the lower corner or corners of a sail to control its position by trimming [see three sheets]

she's long in the tooth though in good shape, a ship is too old for Naval duty, thus, the ship is outdated

shin to skin [shimmy]

ship [1] specifically, a vessel with three or more masts and fully square-rigged throughout

ship [2] any seagoing vessel of one or more masts

ship [3] to stow away oars in a galley, longship, galeota or similar vessel

ship at hull all sails taken in and left to their own devices during high wind, lying ahull

shipboard taking place aboardship

shipman [1] any seaman

shipman [2] a ship's master or commander

ship-of-the-line man-o-war

ship over the stern a wave rolling over the stern or poop in a gale or other storm

ship's articles rules or laws drawn up which pirates sail under and which each pirate must sign upon joining the crew

shipshape tiddley [as are the legendary ships from Bristol], well-organized

'shipshape and Bristol fashion' in first-class order

shipside a dock where a ship loads and unloads passengers and freight

ship's cook often on pirate ships, a deposed captain

ship's manifest invoice of cargo

ship the masts to reinstall masts after they have been struck

shipwright a carpenter skilled in ship construction and repair

shivering the condition of the sails when brought

close to the wind

shiver me timbers! an expression of disbelief or surprise, as when a ship hits a rock or shoal so hard her timbers shake

shoals sandbars at sea near the coast

shoes usually saved for visits ashore

shortsword a sword often used in hand-to-hand combat

shot [1] gun shot of various and sundry sizes and kinds

shot [2] the results of warm work, and by extension, anything proving a failure [Well that's shot then, ain't it Billy Childish?]

shot across the bow a warning shot

shrouds the set of ropes forming part of the rigging and supporting the masts, extending from the masts to the sides of the ship

siege to blockade with impending cannonade

signal gaff a spar for ship's colors

signify to be of import or pertinent to the situation at hand, often used by pirates as a slight against superiors found, or rather captured, on the other side of the law [Yer words don't signify, sirrah!]

silk shirts stolen and only worn for action

Simon the Dancer early 17th century Dutch pirate of the Barbary Coast given the appellation Dali-Capitan or Devil-Captain by the Turks

sink me! an expression of surprise

sirrah sir, but implying inferiority, or derision, to the person addressed as such

skiff a boat with centerboard and spritsail light enough to be rowed

skilly a salt meat and oatmeal broth often served as supper [a fine way to keep up the morale aboardship]

skillygalee [skillygolee] the usual seaman's breakfast drink made of thin, weak broth, or oatmeal porridge boiled in fatty water and sweetened with sugar [another great morale-builder and likely reason for interest in piratical account]

skin [shimmy, shin] to go up or down a mast or canvas

skull and crossbones, the [skull and crossed swords] the feared Black Flag, too, popular images on 17th and 18th century gravestones, leading many to inaccurately believe that those buried there are pirates

skylarking a popular athletic exercise involving racing up and playing in the rigging, often practiced by children and younger men aboardship

slaughterhouse the waist of a ship-o-the-line

slaves a chief pirate booty primarily made up of the Wolof, Bambara, Soso, Mandinka [Mandingo], Kissi, Kru, Dan, Bobo, Adanse, Denkyira, Asante, Akyem, Fante, Fon, Popo, Yoruba, Edo, Igbo, and Efik peoples of West Africa [see panyarr]

slip anchor [slip her cable] to cut cable and leave the anchor on the seabed when there is no time to heave in the cable, or when the crew is too slovenly or drunk to do so, too, to become ill unto death or to die [Ol' Cook's slipped anchor, Cap'n! Canna we do somethin' fer 'im?]

sloop a ship which is fast, agile and has a shallow draft, as large as 100 tons, rigged with a large mainsail attached to a spar above, to the mast on its foremost edge, and to a long boom below, can sport additional sails both square and lateen-rigged, used mainly in the Caribbean and Atlantic, a favorite of pirates, thus, the pirate sloop

sloop-o-war a cruising vessel smaller than a sixth-rate and commanded by both a master and a commander

slop chest a supply of personal goods for sale and charged against the sailor's wage

Ye Olde Seafaring Lexicon

slouch hat a tricorn [tricorner hat] commonly worn by seamen on both sides of the law

slush fund money made from selling in port the fat (slush) from boiled or fried meats aboardship

small bower port bow anchor the same size as the best bower

smallsword the sword preferred by captains, designed to be gentlemanly thrust forward with its point inflicting the deleterious damage

smartly quickly

smelt up when a ship responds favorably [Aye, she smelt up boldly, sir, as we left the cove.]

smother a sail to take a sail down and furl it

snow similar to a brig with two masts, both fully square-rigged but with her spanker set on a separate pole or trysail mast just aft of the mainmast

soft farewell when one pirate ship absconds, usually in the night, from a pirate fleet

son of a gun a manchild conceived in a hammock slung between guns on a ship moored in port, if the child's father is not known, the infant is entered into the ship's log as this

sortie a fever-pitch search by rovers for hidden booty, food, slaves, sex, etc.

soul cages owned by Merrows in which drowned sailors are imprisoned at the bottom of the sea

sound to find the depth of the water

soundings water shallow enough to anchor in

Southern Cross, the looked for in the Southern Hemisphere as a navigational tool

southing to change course south, as to escape storms or ice in the North Atlantic

Spanish Main all Tierra Firme [the mainland originally only along the northern coast of South America] given to Spain by the papal-endorsed Treaty of Tordesillas of June 1494, which is made socially void by the mid-1600's in the race for world domination, eventually becomes all of the romanticized Caribbean [West Indies] and Gulf of Mexico, primarily the land from the Isthmus of Panama to the mouth of the Orinoco River in Venezuela

spanker the gaff sail at the stern, or, the driver or main trysail

spar [1] horizontal beams suspended from the masts, yards, stout wooden poles used for masts or yards, kept in spares on board, as with other gear and utilities

spar [2] a name for the upper deck of a ship

speak with a vessel to take a ship as prize, or, to challenge a ship

specie hard currency such as gold doubloons or silver pieces-of-eight

spend the masts to lose the masts in a storm [The ship hath spent her masts, Tom Dooly, and more's the pity, laddie.]

spice considered excellent booty for its trade value

spill to relieve a sail from the pressure of the wind so as to reef or furl it, or, to relieve the pressure on a sail by coming about or by adjusting the sail with lines

spilling line a line with which to pull in a spritsail

splice to masterfully attach two [or more] ropes together to make one

splice the mainbrace have a drink or three

split when a sail has been blown to pieces

spog a raw recruit

spoom to go before the wind without any sails

spotted dog suet pudding made with flour, sugar, cinnamon, nutmeg, currants, eggs, and milk

spread-eagle a torture where the victim is tied tightly to four stakes in the ground so that he hangs taut between them, not touching the earth below, fires are often then lit below, and/or fuses [matches] are placed between the fingers and toes and then lit, quite a bit tamer than the Norse version, and origination of the name, which has the victim lie face down on a [freezing] flat stone after which his spine is cut away from his ribs, the latter pulled away and thus resembling the wings of an eagle in flight

Spring tides those tides at new and full Moon

spritsail the sail at the bowsprit

spritsail yard a yard set on the underside of the bowsprit to carry the spritsail

spyglass [glass] telescope

squadron a group of warships numbering under 10

squall a gale-force wind or 'cold hurricane' coming down into a ship and making a high-pitched crying sound [squally winds]

square away to square the yards so as to sail before the wind, thus, to put everything into proper order

square meal in the Navy, a hot meal served on a square wooden platter

square-rigged the principal sails set at right angles to the length of the ship and extended by horizontal yards slung to the mast, typical of ancient Egyptian, Mediterranean and Scandinavian [Viking] ships

squeezebox an accordion, often found aboardship

stabbing dagger used in hand-to-hand combat after boarding a vessel

stand away to head out to sea

stand for to come broadside in preparation for warm engagement [She stood for the enemy, and bravely, she did!]

stand off to position a ship, usually to fight

stand off and on [stand in and off] to block another ship by weighing and dropping anchor at different positions

stand out to stand seaward

stand out of the way to go round, as with ice floes

stands away when a ship moves upon her course

stand seaward to chart a course into open water

stands for the offing when the ship stands out to the sea from the shore

stand to anchor across from another ship or a village, etc.

stand with a fair wind to undertake a journey out to sea in perfect sailing weather

starboard [steerboard] the right side of a craft facing forward where, on Viking longships, the ship is operated by an oar turned with a tiller staff, to put to the right

starboard tack changing direction towards the right side of the ship facing the bow by repositioning the sails

starting employing the three sisters on the backs of sailors to make them work faster

statute mile 5,280 feet

stay a large, strong rope used to support a mast or to tighten sails, as in martingale stays

stay-sail a fore-and-aft sail hoisted on a stay

steerage the forward of the stern cabin aneath the quarterdeck

steersman the sailor in charge of the wheel

stem the bowsprit

stem to stern from beginning to end, thus, a thorough job

stepped placed back or aft

stepped mast a lowered mast on some ancient Mediterranean ships, giving room for aboardship battle

stern from the German for star, the back or after part of the ship housing the rudder or wheel and, below that, the captain's quarters which, on pirate ships, is shared with the rowdy crew

sterncastle at the stern ornately carved and housing the poop deck, created in Medieval times for battle at sea

Ye Olde Seafaring Lexicon

stinkpot earthenware pot charged with gunpowder and other combustibles and fitted with a touch-hole, used by pirates as they are boarding, thrown onto the enemy deck or cut from yardarms so as to fall onto the deck of a vessel being attacked, creates great smoke and confusion

stiver a Dutch coin equal to one-twentieth gulden

store ship a ship in a fleet filled with provisions

storm to overwhelm with ground troops

stowaway an unwanted voyager

strappado [Spanish] a torture where both arms are pulled behind the back and tied, and then the body is suspended from a rope and pulley attached to a gallows-like arm, the victim then is dropped until just before he hits the ground, this done repeatedly until the victim dies [see trice up]

stream any ocean current

strike to run aground

strike colors [strike to] lower the ship's colors in surrender

strike masts to dismantle the ship's masts, a laborious process taking many hours

strike sail to lower sails in surrender

strung up hanged

studding sail the sail extending beyond the side of the edge of a square sail, used to make the most of light winds

sudden precipitation into the other world an unexpected death

suet tallow [hard fat] from kidneys and loins in beef and mutton

Suffolk cheese common Navy cheese eventually replaced by Cheshire and Gloucester, viz., Hunger could break through anything except Suffolk cheese, or,
Mocks the weak effort
of the bending blade,

or in the hog-trough
rests in perfect spite,
too big to swallow,
and too hard to bite

sugar king of exports from the Caribbean

sun dried hanged

sunset take the wind a positive hope of a gale wind dying at sunset

supercargo the commercial officer of the cargo of a merchant pink, often the primary captive of pirates because of his knowledge of the cargo aboard

superior above [The cargo superior to the bales of cotton wast rifled through.]

supper made up of leftovers from dinner

supply ship a consort ship carrying supplies for long voyages

surf-boat a small boat carrying a complement of 10

swab [swabbie] disrespectful term for a sailor, a swab is type of mop made out of rope-yarns or threads, therefore, a person who mops the decks using the swab is often called, and derogatorily, swabbie

swag loot

swain [Old English] boy [as in boatswain, bosun, or boat-boy]

swallow the anchor to retire from life at sea and settle down ashore

swashbuckler a 16th century name for any brigand, land or sea, first used in writings of the 16th century, it refers to any warrior making a loud noise by striking his sword against his shield

sweat the tying of a man to the mizzenmast between decks, setting lighted candles all round the mast and then communally running round said mast sticking and pricking the unfortunate with penknives, tucks, forks, compasses, etc., this torture lasts for 10-12 minutes, and is not designed to kill

Ye Olde Seafaring Lexicon

sweating when a victim is forced to run round a mast at spearpoint until he passes out

sweep a long oar used by any large vessel utilizing oars

swing at the anchor to wait, anchored, for a favorable wind

swing the lead a lead weight swung from a line into water when near shore was a way to measure depth, the job's simple requirements causes the phrase to evolve into a term for slacking off [Aye, Jim Black's swingin' the lead again, Tom.]

swivel gun a small cannon set on the rail of a ship which can be moved from side to side

T

tack to change course by turning the bow into the wind until the wind blows on the other side of the vessel and the ship takes the opposite but same angle, to turn

taffrail the ornately-carved rail at the sterncastle behind the wheelbox

take a caulk the deck's gaps are sealed with oakum and tar, and napping on them leaves black lines on the clothes, a sailor going to nap on deck can say he's going to 'take a caulk'

take in sail to roll up all sails

take lie of the land to move onto new wilderness cautiously, or to take initial care in a new village or city, so as to discern native customs and the whereabouts of libation, sustenance, and other creature-comforts

taken aback when a sailing ship is facing unexpectedly into the wind, thus, taken by surprise

take the wind out o' their sails overbear

tar [1] pine extract residue used to waterproof clothes and to dress pigtails, which is the reason for the protective flap at the back of the Navy sailors' uniform

tar [2] affectionate dysphemism for any seaman

tartan [Arabic] a two-masted variant of the galeota, an Arabic ship which is fast, maneuverable and narrow, sports one mast with a lateen mainsail and a small foresail on her bowsprit, carries 30 oars, sometimes a small mizzenmast is added with a lateen rig, used primarily in the Mediterranean

taunt a ship with very high masts and narrow sails, but because of this is subject to wringing

taut the maritime word for tight [He's a taut hand,

meaning 'He's a stern disciplinarian.']

'tell it to the marines' a phrase revealing the naivety of British marines in regard to their believing tall tales that hardened sailors would see to be untrue

tender a small vessel attending a larger craft and used to ferry people from ship to ship or from ship to shore, most often towed at stern

Terra Australis Incognita [Latin] unexplored Australia and Antarctica

Tethys [Greek] the sea, after the most supreme of sea goddesses

the devil to pay to caulk, or pay, the difficult-to-get-at devil seam of the ship

'The Devil's beatin' his wife' a sunshower, or when the sun shines while it is raining

thieves watch nine o'clock post meridian

Thomas Cocklyn elected captain 'due to his brutality and ignorance'

Thomas Tew aka the 'Rhode Island Pirate,' a 17th century English privateer-turned-pirate, meets a bloody death on the latter of only two journeys, pioneers the route which becomes known as the 'Pirate Round,' many other pirates, including Henry Every and William Kidd, will follow in his path, his flag has a black field and a white arm wielding a cutlass

three sheets to the wind very drunk, one sheet can trim a sail, the implication that the seaman is so inebriated that even with 3 sheets he can't trim a sail

three sisters three pieces of rattan bound together with waxed twine and used indiscriminately by masters-at-arms and botswain's mates in the practice called starting, named after the most feared Celtic portent of doom where Ana, Macha and Badhbh [or Nemhain] appear before warriors on the eve of a great slaughter

tiddley neat, tidy

tide over the original 'tiding over' is a seafaring term and derives from 'tide' being synonymous with 'time', the literal meaning being 'in the absence of wind to fill the sails, float with the tide', thus, take what you have until there is more or the time is right

tide race the leeward tide [dangerous for ships but excellent for landing parties]

tierce one-third pipe, or 42 gallons

tiller the lever fitted into the head of a rudder and used for turning it

tiller ropes used to steer a vessel

tobacco chewed more often than smoked, smoking being forbidden below deck, a major New World export

to each his own the last command of the captain when a pirate company breaks gang

topgallant sail the sail above the topsail, or the third sail in ascending order from the deck

topsail a sail set on the topmast above the mainsail, or the second sail in ascending order from the deck

tornado a hurricane

touch and go the nerve-wracking situation when a ship's keel touches or brushes a shoal but does not become grounded, thus, by extension, to hover between life and death

touch-hole the hole on a gun where the fire is touched to the fuse

touch off a batch of orphans masturbate

Trade Winds strong easterly winds which blow through the tropics and subtropics

traffick cargo

transported with passion to be beside oneself with murderous anger

travado [Spanish] along the African coast, a sudden and hard gust of wind accompanied by thunder, lightning and heavy showers

Ye Olde Seafaring Lexicon

Treaty of Whitehall, the [1686] decreed that
conflict in the New World will not lead to war
between Britain and France, thus giving free rein to
privateers of both nations

trice up a torture where the victim is hauled into the
rigging and then let fall over and over, usually until
his bones are all broken or he is dead

trim [trimming] to set a sail

tuck [1] the part of the vessel where the ends of the
lower planks meet under the stern

tuck [2] a rapier

tucked up hanged

Turgut a Turkish corsair and Ottoman admiral
during the mid-16th century

turn to tack

turned off the scaffold hanged

turn in go to sleep, retire

turn in all standing to turn in fully dressed during a
storm or in expectation of conflict

twaqo [Malay] Malaysian junk

twelve pounder a cannon that fires 12 lb. balls

ult. [Latin] the abbreviation for ultimo, meaning the previous month

under the weather a crewman standing watch on the weather, or windward [opposite of leeward], side of the bow is subject to the constant beating of the sea, therefore, the ill condition often caused from standing such a watch

under way when a ship enjoys movement through the water

unsafe [n.] a region not safe for a pirate hideout [That'd be an unsafe if'n I ever did see one, sir.]

unwarranted not legal according to the job description of a Navy warrant officer

up in arms ready for an engagement

upperworks rails, gunwales, foredeck, quarterdeck, castles

used abused, tortured

vail to lower sails in submission or salute

Valefor the fiend appearing as a many-headed lion who leads those he is familiar with into theft

veer to slacken cordage

Venetian frigate a small oared boat ca. 35 feet in length and 7 feet wide

Vepar the fiend who appears as a Mermaid, creates storms at sea and causes the same to appear full of ships, occasions death in three days by means of putrefying sores and worm-eaten wounds

victuals [vittles] 'belly timber,' food

viking [Scandinavian] from vik, meaning bay, to go viking signifies to cross a bay by boat, land and maraud at will, later, Viking[s], broadly, any Teutonisch seafarers to include Angles, Saxons, Jutes [Danes], Frisians, etc.

Vitalian Brotherhood a company of privateers later turning to piracy, hired in 1392 by the Dukes of Mecklenburg to fight against Denmark because the Danish Queen Margaret I had imprisoned Albrecht of Mecklenburg and his son in order to subdue the kingdom of Sweden, from 1392 onward, they were a power to be reckoned with in the Baltic Sea, had safe harbors in the cities of Rostock, Ribnitz, Stralsund, and Wismar, soon go their own way, turning to open piracy and coastal robbery, in 1393 they sack the town of Bergen, and in 1394 they conquer Malmö, they too plunder Åbo, Vyborg, Faxeholm, Styresholm, and Korsholm, and occupy parts of Frisia and Schleswig, at the climax of their power, they occupy Gotland in 1394 and set up their headquarters in Visby, because of them, Baltic Sea maritime trade collapses, and the herring industry

suffers from their ravages

waft [wiff] a hoisted flag rolled up or tied in a knot and used as a distress signal or as a sign of mockery by pirates

waggoner a sea atlas, or volumes of navigation charts originally created by studying stolen Portuguese maps, the Portuguese being some of the first navigators, but losing out in the arms race to rule the world

waggoners o' the sea Dutch pirates of the Dutch East India Company, Sea Beggars

waist the center of a deck between the fore and aft decks, often unrailed

waister a seaman employed in waist of ship, and so by extension, an untrained or incompetent seaman

walking the plank a deadly punishment where the victim has his hands and feet tied and then is marched along a plank set on the rail of the ship, rarely employed, if ever, some documents show that when food is scarce with none in sight, slaves are made to throw themselves overboard in this or a similar fashion

warm engagement close and fierce hand-to-hand combat

warm work heated battle

warp [to warp up] to move or maneuver a vessel in restricted waters by heaving her along with ropes [warps] attached to piles, posts, trees or buoys

warp out o' the straight of a ship, to become old and bent, of a man, to become strange and selfish, or even devious [Ol' Cap'n Stagg wast warped complete out o' the straight afore he slipped anchor, Tom.]

watch the duty of watching for sails, the enemy, approaching storms, ne'er-do-wells in port, etc.

waterway a groove at the edge of the ship's deck for draining whatever might need to be drained

way a ship's movement through the water

wear an' lay to upon the other tack for hurricane conditions, to continually veer [wear] ship [wind at stern] and then to bring her bow about into the wind and hold her stationary at either starboard or port before tacking again and beginning the process over, i.e., to keep the ship first with the wind aft and then fore so that the end result is essentially a war with the storm so the ship won't be capsized by continuous gusts and water to one part of the ship or another

weather gauge a ship lying to windward of another

wear ship [veer ship] to cause a square-rigged ship to course with the wind to the stern, put her on the other tack by turning away from the wind, equivalent of gybing in fore-and-aft rigged vessels, to move the bow in the direction of the wind

weather lore usually put into rhyme, observations concerning the weather trusted by seamen to give an accurate presage; example:

Red sky at night, sailor's delight.
Red sky in morning, sailor take warning.

weatherly able for all weather

weathermost usually describing safe harbor on an island ['Twas a weathermost isle, b'God!]

weigh to pull up anchor, weigh anchor

weighted line used to sound the depth of the water, measured with marks, or colored pieces of cloth or leather attached to the line [ex: mark twain]

welcoming hoist flags of welcome at port

wench derogatory term for a girl

Western Sea the Atlantic Ocean

West Indies the Caribbean

Ye Olde Seafaring Lexicon

W. G. Perrin Jolly Roger [flag historian] a black skeleton on a yellow field

wheel [steering wheel] adopted in the late 17th century, replacing the unwieldy tiller, operates the all-important rudder of the ship via a series of block-and-tackle rigs below the wheelbox

wheelbox the location of the wheel in the sterncastle

whipstaff an extended tiller for the helmsman to work the rudder by remote control

whistling a superstition to bring wind, a fearful act reserved for the captain and quartermaster

white shirts very commonly worn by pirate crews as a show of force and solidarity, possibly instituted by the well-loved and respected commodore Howell Davis of the Le Bouse/Cocklyn/Davis Piratick Confederacy

whole nine yards all three masts of a ship-of-the-line full and ready for combat, until the opponent 'goes the whole nine yards,' she is not yet dedicated to engage [She'll need to go the whole nine yards, now, but we've got her. Fire!]

Who'll go? the common question posed by a pirate captain to his crew concerning who will volunteer to do this or that, including drawing straws to become ghost-sentry of buried treasure

William de Briggeho the first recorded Norman-English pirate executed by his government in 1228

William Fly an English pirate captain who raids New England shipping until he is captured by the crew of a seized ship, hanged in Boston, Fly approaches his hanging with complete disdain and even reproaches the hangman for doing a poor job, remaking the noose and placing it about his neck with his own two hands

William Kidd [Captain Kidd] pirate most famous for his alleged egregious acts on the high seas while privateering, hanged May 23, 1701 at Execution

Ye Olde Seafaring Lexicon

Dock, at Wapping

Wimund a Scottish bishop who becomes a sea-faring war-lord in the years after 1147

wind the point of the compass where the ship's head lies [How does the ship wind?]

windage the extent to which a ship is blown off course by the wind

windfall wind blowing from a leeshore, giving the ship more leeway

windlass [capstan] a wench-like horizontal rotating barrel supported on vertical poles and turned by a crank so the hoisting rope is wound round the barrel

wind of ball a major cause of death when a cannon ball flies by a sailor close to his stomach, but does not hit him; it is assumed that the ball hits his 'spiritual' outer shell and thus causes internal, physical damage [flying by the head rarely causes damage]

windward the weather side of the ship, opposite of leeward, or landward

windward-eyed when a sailor keeps an eye open to windward, the direction from which the weather comes

wing to disable with cannon shot some principal function of a ship, such as a mast, sail, or rudder

Wōkòu Japanese pirates

wooden walls a euphemism for a ship seeming to be like a prison

woolen breeches worn on both land and sea

wore to veer away from the wind so that it blows from astern

work [v.] the act of managing the sails

working the alarming movement of a bowsprit, yard, or mast in a storm

working to windward when the wind is before a ship's sails

wringing [all-a-taunt-o] when a ship twists,

shortening her life considerably [I never see'd anything like it, matey! She wast all-a-taunt-o!]

Y

Yannig an uncanny thing that emerges from the sea at night, hooting like a wounded owl, no human should ever heed its pitiful calls, for the third will be behind the person's back, and this creature will then consume him or turn him into a whiff of air

yard a spar suspended from the mast to extend the sails, most masts carry three of these

yardarm either end of a yard

yare easy to handle, responding quickly and accurately to the helm [Aye, she's yare, she be, a right beauty— an' savvy on the open sea!]

yarn a tale, or, [v.] to tell tall tales of bravery and adventure, ghost stories and fables, legends, etc.

yawl a fore-and-aft rigged sailboat carrying a mainsail and one or more jibs with a mizzenmast far aft

yestreen [Anglo-Scot] yesterday evening, last night

yo ho! be attentive

younkers the young foremastmen

Piratic Articles

1. "Every man shall have an equal vote in affairs of moment. He shall have an equal title to the fresh provisions or strong liquors at any time seized, and shall use them at pleasure unless a scarcity makes it necessary for the common good that a retrenchment may be voted."

2. "Every man shall be called fairly in turn by the list on board of prizes, because over and above their proper share, they are allowed a shift of clothes. But if they defraud the company to the value of even one dollar in plate, jewels, or money, they shall be marooned. If any man rob another, he shall have his nose and ears slit, and be put ashore where he shall be sure to encounter hardships."

3. "None shall game for money, either with dice or cards."

4. "The lights and candles shall be put out at eight at night, and if any of the crew desire to drink after that hour they shall sit upon the open deck without lights."

5. "Each man shall keep his piece, cutlass and pistols, at all times clean and ready for action."

6. "No boy or woman shall be allowed amongst them. If any man shall be found seducing one of the latter sex and carrying her to sea in disguise, he shall suffer death."

7. "He that shall desert the ship or his quarters in the time of battle shall be punished by death or marooning."

8. "None shall strike another on board the ship, but every man's quarrel shall be

ended onshore by sword or pistol in this manner: at the word of command from the Quartermaster, each man being previously placed back to back, shall turn and fire immediately. If any man do not, the Quartermaster shall knock the piece out of his hand. If both miss their aim, they shall take to their cutlasses, and he that draws first blood shall be declared the victor."

9. "Every man who shall become a cripple or lose a limb in the service shall have eight hundred pieces of eight from the common stock, and for lesser hurts proportionately."

10. "The Captain and the Quartermaster shall each receive two shares of a prize, the Master Gunner and Boatswain, one and one half shares, all other officers one and one quarter, and private gentlemen of fortune one share each."

Ye Olde Seafaring Lexicon

11. "The musicians shall have rest on the Sabbath Day only, by right, on all other days, by favor only."

12. "No child found yet in innocence shall be harmed by any man aboardship, on pain of death."

Ye Olde Seafaring Lexicon

The Son of God Chantey

Lord Jesus was a sailorman—
  no man would venture out
too many leagues away from land
  depending on a shout
back to the shore where children there
  might hear yet stand aghast,
their little fingers spread in fear
  as Jesus cried 'Avast! The mast!'
    As Jesus cried 'Avast!'

He walked on water, hindered sleets,
  but not to save His life!
He could have danced upon the sheets
  playing a happy fife.
He knew the ropes, did taste the winds
  to see if these were fair.
The things below were all His friends,
  as well the fowl of air.
    The air! Up there!
    Where wing the foul and fair!

A storm blew up on Galilee,
  threatening the fishing craft,
the Lord cried 'Down helm easterly!
  Ho! Lively there abaft!
    Afore! And aft!
    Look smart now! Don't be daft!'

So sing we, when ye venture out
upon the rolling waves,
O, ne'er set sail your ship in doubt,
even if Jesus saves!
  Us knaves! He saves!
  Right out our watery graves!
  Yo-Ho!

A Note On Piracy

In all but a few novel cases, most pirates, aside from being stricken with that which pirate aficionado Jack Beeching identifies as thing-fever, are extremely violent and bloodthirsty. Yet, because of horrendous authoritarian views and practices having found their way into every nook and cranny of modern life, piracy, and especially that of the Golden Age, has become--for many-- the perfect symbol for fun-loving, peaceful anarchy; and this probably in large part because the actual character of the average pirate is in reality so heinous that his [or her] caricature gathers up the "good" qualities while dispensing with the monstrous which, truthfully, are no different than those carried by government agents licensed to kill. Respectable morality and indecorous immorality are two sides of the same coin, and so pirates, sensing this, are unable to know what to do with the liberating information and sadly choose the less legalistic and more duplicitous of the two sides. It would seem, then, that the pirate is the conscience of the entire legal system, without the wherewithal, for whatever reasons, to step outside of the dominant paradigm and turn to look at the injustices dispassionately and with the lofty but attainable goal of personal, nonviolent freedom. Captivatingly, the aforementioned Beeching, who writes the introduction to the 1969 edition of the riveting and oftentimes gratuitously violent classic by Alexander O. Exquemelin entitled The

Buccaneers of America (first published in 1678) states that the pirate is "not only a fantasy figure for today's cautiously ethical businessman, but his exact historical progenitor." Well, let us not be too quick in our own inequitable day with the word ethical, but we have every reason in the world to agree with Beeching when he posits that the pirate is the direct social ancestor of the multinational capitalist; the quintessential American businessman... which of course includes the career politician, the church leader, and the real estate entrepreneur, among other dubious purveyors of the postwar dream.

Scáth Beorh

December 2006

About This Book

Ye OLDE SEAFARING LEXICON had its beginning in 1972 as a list of piracy terms collected by then 9-year-old Scáth Beorh, the present editor of this volume. Nothing, short of a dozen or so words, ever came of said list. In 1993 while Beorh attended Flagler College in St. Augustine, Florida, his English Literature class read Gulliver's Travels by Irish writer Jonathan Swift. As Beorh read, he was amazed at how many terms Swift routinely uses which are identical to those used by his father Milledge L. Cooper of the Cooper Basin located just north of Ferry Pass, a settlement found in the northeastern section of Pensacola, Florida. A decade later Ye OLDE SEAFARING LEXICON was begun, and was completed in its present provisional form in 2014 — 42 years from its inception.

Ye Olde Seafaring Lexicon

Books Published by

CREEPING LIGHT PRESS

Ye Olde Seafaring Lexicon

Mistress of the Devil

The Autobiography of Gemma Galgani

Horror Flicks

October House

Horror & The Christian

Wildflower Prayer Journal

Haunted By Benevolence

Yewley's Good & Evil Monsters

For Strangers & Exiles

A Selected Annotated Bibliography

Ashdown, Peter. <u>Caribbean History In Maps</u>. Trinidad and Jamaica: Longman Group Limited, Longman Caribbean, 1979. This work is extremely precise, made up mostly of maps with informative text. This is a recommended book for anyone studying the colorful history of the still-burgeoning Caribbean.

Chesney, Kellow. <u>The Victorian Underworld</u>. London: The History Book Club, 1970. A dry but informative volume detailing the history of the underworld made famous by Charles Dickens, this study carries the one perk of an often ribald dictionary of Victorian street slang.

Cordingly, David. <u>Under the Black Flag: The Romance and the Reality of Life Among the Pirates</u>. New York: Random House, 1996. This is a quick and informative read covering all ideas about piracy from straight history to the silver screen. Cordingly is a good scholar and certainly knows his field, even able to debunk a contemporary position that most [if not all] pirates practiced homosexuality.

Defoe, Daniel. <u>A General History of the Robberies and Murders of the Most Notorious Pyrates, and also Their Policies, Discipline and Government</u>. London: J. M. Dent & Sons, 1972. Originally published in 1724. A massive work requiring much time to plough through, but well worth the trouble, this study is considered a classic in the field of Piracy.

Ye Olde Seafaring Lexicon

Exquemelin, Alexander O. <u>The Buccaneers of America.</u> [Unabridged]. Harmondsworth, England: Penguin Books, 1969. Originally published in 1678. Often gratuitously violent, this book remains a very well-written classic, and holds the distinction of being, as far as we know, the only published book on piracy written by an actual pirate.

Johnson, Captain Charles. <u>A General History of the Robberies & Murders of the Most Notorious Pyrates</u>. London: Conway Maritime Press, 1998. Originally published in 1724. If nothing else, this volume is an extremely fun read and indispensable for the pirate library. Johnson turns a phrase not unlike the most droll comedian. Both Robert Louis Stevenson and J. M. Barrie studied this work before writing their children's classics Treasure Island and Peter Pan, respectively.

Kemp, Peter, Editor. <u>The Oxford Companion to Ships and the Sea</u>. Oxford: Oxford University Press, 1976. This enormous encyclopedia is verily worth its weight in doubloons. No maritime research should be undertaken without the help of this masterpiece.

Konstam, Angus. <u>The History of Pirates</u>. Guilford, Connecticut: The Lyons Press, 1999. Lively and packed with full-color illustrations, this coffee-table-like book is an essential in piratical study.

Marine Research Society. <u>The Pirates Own Book, or Authentic Narratives of the Lives, Exploits and Executions of the Most Celebrated Sea Robbers</u>. [MRS Publication Number Four] Salem, Massachusetts:

Ye Olde Seafaring Lexicon

Marine Research Society, 1924. Originally published in 1837. A thick work, this book is worth the study nonetheless. Unknown pirates captains and little known types of sea banditti are discussed here in great detail.

McCarthy, Kevin M. Twenty Florida Pirates. Sarasota, Florida: Pineapple Press, Inc., 1994. Seemingly written for children, this fun and extremely informative work brings the reader as far as 1993 CE with piratical exploit.

Rediker, Marcus. Between the Devil and the Deep Blue Sea: Merchant Seamen, Pirates and the Anglo-American Maritime World, 1700-1750. Cambridge: Cambridge University Press, 1987. This is a scholarly series of maritime essays. The entire book is pertinent to the subject of piracy, but the chapters entitled 'The Seaman as the 'Spirit of Rebellion'' and 'The Seaman as Pirate' answer some of the perplexing questions concerning piracy.

Seitz, Don [Sir] Carlos. Under the Black Flag: Exploits of the Most Notorious Pirates. New York: The Dial Press, 1925. Many corsairs not found in the Pirate Pantheon, where Blackbeard and Black Bart comfortably reside, are looked at here in surprising detail. This book is an absolute must for the pirate aficionado.

Ships' Miscellany: A Guide to the Royal Navy of Jack Aubrey. Editor made anonymous. London: Michael O'Mara Books Ltd., 2003. This entertaining and instructive volume holds much information concerning the British Royal Navy from 1793-1815, and is based on the historically accurate fictional works of Patrick O'Brian.

Spraggs, Gillian. <u>Outlaws & Highwaymen: The Cult of the Robber in England from the Middle Ages to the Nineteenth Century</u>. London: Pimlico [Random House], 2001. Notwithstanding many overwritten quasi-intellectual sections, this book tackles a topic not often written about, which makes it a gem in the library of the historian of European history. Highly-rarefied studies range chronologically from the precursors of Robin Hood to Dick Turpin.

Stephens, John Richard, Editor. <u>Captured By Pirates: 22 Firsthand Accounts of Murder and Mayhem on the High Seas</u>. Cambria, California: Fern Canyon Press, 1996. This book is a brutally honest anthology where actual encounters are revealed, some for the first time since their publication during the Golden Age. A wild and often gory ride, this collection should not be studied on a full stomach.

Villiers, Captain Alan. <u>Men, Ships and the Sea</u>. New Edition. Washington, D.C.: National Geographic Society, 1973. Originally published in 1962. The concise history of all things maritime, this book, written by the man who captained the Mayflower II across the Atlantic in 1957, is requisite to any study of the high seas.

Ye Olde Seafaring Lexicon

Waterbury, Jean Parker, Editor. <u>The Oldest City</u>. St. Augustine, Florida: The St. Augustine Historical Society, First Edition, Fourth Printing, 1983. A beautifully done history of the oldest European city in the New World, this book is requisite for any student of St. Augustine.

Ye Olde Seafaring Lexicon

What's a pirate's favorite letter?
The Letter of Marque.
I like that letter much better than Rrrrrgh!
which sounds like you are joking,
or maybe even choking,
or could be you are poking a shark.
In any case, you're missing the marque.